Journal of the International Relations and Affairs Group (JIRAG)
Volume II, Issue II
December 2012

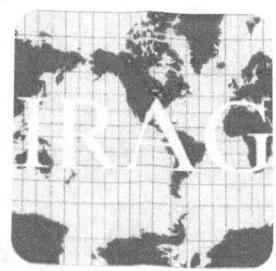

Journal of the International Relations and Affairs Group (JIRAG)

Volume II, Issue II

December 2012

Journal of the International Relations and Affairs Group (JIRAG)

The International Relations and Affairs Group supports research in foreign affairs and global issues among states within the international system, including the roles of states, inter-governmental organizations (IGOs), non-governmental organizations (NGOs), and multinational corporations (MNCs). We focus on geopolitical analysis, globalization, and international policy issues and apply qualitative and quantitative analysis. Our focus is analyzing, as well as formulating solutions to issues with foreign policy, cultural interaction, crisis and other. We have a network of over 16,500 members globally. The group can be found on LinkedIn at:

http://www.linkedin.com/company/international-relations-and-affairs-group

And online at:

http://www.intlrelationsandaffairs.com

JIRAG welcomes submissions on the following topics: Geopolitical Analysis, Homeland Security, National Security, Globalization, Conflict Resolution, Commerce, Law, Diplomacy, Intelligence Community, Negotiation, Government, Defense, Warfare, Business, Public Policy, Terrorism, Crime, Economic Trade, NGO's, MNC's, Disaster, Culture, Human Trafficking and other related topics.

JIRAG publishes a winter and Spring Edition each year.

Submissions may be made to: info@intlrelationsandaffairs.com

JIRAG ©2012

Dawn Marie Evans
Editor

Mrs. Evans is a Senior Consultant at IBM/SPSS and is a Managing Partner at Evans Analytics. She has over 15 years of research experience in both quantitative and qualitative research. Mrs. Evans manages projects, conducts statistical modeling and programming assignments. She is expert in SAS and SPSS programming and statistics, text analytics, and data mining. She also sits on the editorial board of the Qualitative Report, a peer reviewed qualitative research journal, in which she has also published grounded theory research. She has also published quantitatively and qualitatively in top-tier national journals.

Education:

MS, Advanced Analytics, North Carolina State University, Raleigh, NC, 2010

MS, Family Therapy, Nova Southeastern University, Fort Lauderdale, FL, May, 1997

BS, Family Science, minor Psychology, Brigham Young University, Provo, UT, 1991

Nannan ZHAO
Associate Editor

Nannan's first language is Chinese but also speaks English and German. She has had courses in politics, law, computer science, and e-business. She has been a volunteer in activities, such as, About Old House in Shanghai, and Mid-Autumn Dream Gala; the former was held by the National Tourism Administration of The People's Republic of China, and the latter was held by Shanghai Municipal Tourism Administration. As a volunteer she was responsible for introducing the history of buildings. She believes studying politics give an understanding of human history, activities, and ideology, as well as, philosophy and cultural system.

Education:

MA, in International Relations (Middle East), Durham University

Diploma, in Global Politics, Business, and Academic English, Queen Mary, University of London

BA, in English, Shanghai Jiao Tong University

Nashiru Abdulai
Associate Editor

Nashiru is Ghanaian, and a FSO with the Passport Office of the Ministry of Foreign Affairs and Regional Integration, Accra-Ghana. He effectively works with colleagues from various cultures and professional backgrounds.

Education:

Executive MBA, candidate, Kwame Nkrumah University of Science and Technology

BBA, Banking and Finance, University of Ghana

Damian Corbet
Associate Editor

Damian is a Senior press officer at Halma p.l.c., a UK where he is responsible for the global PR activities of some of the subsidiaries, and coordinates the PR output of all Halma's companies in China and India. He is interested in global issues and has written commentaries for OOSKA news, an influential, US-based newsletter covering water in the developing world. He occasionally writes freelance press releases for B2B clients in industries as diverse as food processing and facilities management.

Education:

MA, Global Politics, Birkbeck, University of London

BSc, Biological Science, University of East Anglia

Elisabeth Morris-Maragoula
Associate Editor

Elisabeth has over eleven years of experience managing communications outreach and negotiations globally, coordinating international publications and projects, researching a wide range of policy issues, pitching and developing fresh communication strategies, and editing and writing news and key documents.

Education:

MA, International Relations & Diplomacy, Schiller International University, Paris

BA, Economics (major), Italian language (minor), University of California, Los Angeles

---

Teddy Lishan Desta, PhD
Associate Editor

Dr. Desta has worked as a lecturer at Alemaya University, and later as an accountant at PepsiCo, Inc. Currently, Dr. Desta works as a teaching assistant for FIU. His specialties are finance and accounting, teaching and coaching, social and economic research, data analysis, and ideation.

Education:

PhD, International Relations, the University of Texas at Dallas

MSc, Economics, Baylor University

MSc, Agricultural Development, University College Dublin

BSc, Agricultural Economics, Alemaya University

Table of Contents

Role of NGOs in the Pre-WTO International Trading System

Nimisha Pandey, Ph.D. (Thesis Submitted)

Abstract

Post Second World War era marked the development of international trading system that embodied in the form of GATT/WTO based on inter-state system. Since, sovereign states were the sole legitimate actors in the field of international trade, Non-Governmental Organizations (NGOs) as main component of civil society had negligible presence in the international trading system as the trade and civil society regime each developed in their own domain and preoccupation with less desire and opportunities to interact with each other. The GATT did not institutionalize any relationship with NGOs. However, traditional actors pursuing interests of specific sector such as business and industrial groups had a historical role to play in the field of trade because of their stakes in the trade policy. The presence and mobilization of NGOs in the field of international trade have heightened with the growing importance of globalization and liberalization in 1990s and thereby expansion of international trade agenda including new areas such as intellectual property rights, services that affected public interests issues like public health, environment represented by NGOs. Hence, unlike the GATT, the WTO as multilateral trade organization has constituted some provisions for NGOs involvement in the organization working process that has been impacted the dynamics of international trade negotiations and rule making agenda of states.

Introduction

The central objective of the article is to examine the evolution of the role that Non-Governmental Organizations (NGOs) have played in the international trading system. The international trading system embodied in the General Agreement on Tariffs and Trade (GATT)/World Trade Organization (WTO) is based on inter-state system representing states' trade and commercial interests. During the Cold War period, NGOs pursuing public interest issues[1] such as public health, environment, human rights; were less involved in the international trading system because the GATT as international trade negotiating forum had not institutionalized any relationship with NGOs as well as NGOs had less focus and interests in the field of international trade. 1990 onwards, with the increased significance of globalization and liberalization, trade expanded across the world and impacted the public interests issues. This stimulated NGOs to pay attention to the field of international trade.

There are many actors in the field of international trade policy. Workers, consumers, firms and those with commercial interests have a direct stake in trade as trade affects their wages and investment. These traditional actors in trade policy are represented through industrial lobbies, trade unions, exporter or importer associations and consumer advocacy organizations. In addition to these traditional actors in trade policy, there are also a number of new actors in trade policy such as environmentalists, advocates for labour standards, human rights activists and others. These groups perceive a link between their respective issues and trade, either through trade's direct impact on their issue or possibly through the use of trade sanctions as a mechanism.

The Uruguay Round of Trade Negotiations (1986-1994) expanded the international trade agenda by including new issues such as agriculture, services and intellectual property rights (IPRs) that had an impact on the public interest issues such as environment, labour, human right and public health etc. With this development, several NGOs for instance, *Oxfam, Care International, Greenpeace* etc. started to pay keener attention to international trade and demanded for their participation in trade policy debate. Consequently, the WTO as main multilateral trade organization established in 1995 and added some provisions for NGOs

---

[1] Public interest issues refer to those issues that are related to the welfare of common people.

participation in its constitution. The increased visibility of NGOs in the field of international trade and their desire to participate in trade policy debate raised many questions regarding the nature of involvement (whether formal or informal) of NGOs in the international trade negotiations and its implications. Would the interaction of NGOs with the international trade negotiation forum exclusively related to commercial interests, be detrimental to international trading system?

While NGOs involvement in the field of international trade institutionally begins since the establishment of the WTO in 1995, discussion over NGOs interaction with international trading system had started since the 'Second World War' with the beginning of negotiation process for the establishment of International Trade Organization (ITO). Hence, subsequent section seeks to take into account the role of NGOs at the interface of international trading system starting from the ITO Havana Charter till the establishment of the WTO in 1995.

Involvement of NGOs in the Multilateral Trade Negotiations

The international trade policy began to be regulated after the establishment of post-Second World War institutional arrangements when GATT was established in 1947. 1945 onwards, the established international trading system was based on liberal concept of trade and considered as an alternative to the protectionist trade regime that evolved in the inter-war period. In terms of role of NGOs in the field of international trade, there was almost negligible involvement of NGOs in the trade policy debate due to the lack of legislative provisions for NGOs' participation in international institutions. The increased visibility of NGOs as participants in the trade policy debate can be seen with the increased significance of the neo-liberal economic globalization in 1990s. Although NGOs did not participate in the international trade negotiations post-World War II, a significant role was planned for NGOs to play in international trading system by developed countries especially by the US and UK. .

The UN Conference on Trade and Employment (1946-48) and Debates regarding NGOs' role in the ITO Charter

The United States began to put its efforts to shape the international trade regime into a new institutional form in order to have economic stability at the international level after World War II. The US and its allies decided to create a stable and liberal international economic order based on principles embedded in the UN Charter. The UN was formed in 1945 and its subordinate body ECOSOC at its first meeting in 1946 adopted a resolution calling for a conference to draft a charter for an International Trade Organization (Jackson 1997: 36). US prepared the *Suggested Charter for an International Trade Organization* for consideration at the *United Nations Conference on Trade and Employment (1946-48)* that would codify and monitor a set of specific trade rules. In its Suggested Charter for the ITO, the US proposed Article 71 entitled 'Relations with Other Organizations' for consideration on the role NGOs would play in the ITO (Deese 2008: 41). The US went a step ahead of the UN Charter by proposing in Article 71 (ITO 1949: 352):

> "The organization may make suitable arrangements for consultation and cooperation with non-governmental organizations concerned with matters within its competence, and may invite them to undertake specific tasks". [2]

In early 1946, the US tabled a resolution to call for an International Conference on Trade and Employment and for a Preparatory Committee to have a discussion on the Suggested Charter. This resolution was adopted and the first session of the Preparatory Committee was assembled in London in October 1946 (Wilson 1947: 127). During the First Session, the US took an initiative to amend the rules of procedure to provide NGOs access to the London meeting. Consequently, NGOs seeking consultative status were identified and listed in the new rules of procedure for the preparatory committee. The listed NGOs were the *World Federation of Trade Unions, the International Co-operative Alliance (ICA),* the *American Federation of Labour* and the *International Chamber of Commerce (ICC)* (Charnovitz and Wickham 1995: 113).

It has been observed that during post Second World War, traditional associations of workers, consumers, labourers, farmers; and of those with commercial interests like industrial groups had direct stakes in the trade policy debate as trade affected their wages and investment policies. Apart from these traditional actors in trade policy, new actors such as environmentalists, human rights and others did not have any stakes in trade policy negotiations as they did not perceive any direct link with trade issues (Jones 2004:168).

---

[2] Article 71 of the UN Charter provided "the UN Economic and Social Council may make suitable arrangements for *consultation* with non-governmental organizations which are concerned with matters within its competence".

The US later presented its working paper to clear the difference between the ITO provisions and the UN Charter provision on NGOs. The UN Charter provision contemplates relations with international as well as national NGOs. "The drafters of the Suggested Charter seemingly thought that national NGOs would influence the ITO through their respective national delegations, whereas international NGOs would have direct involvement with the ITO" (Charnovitz and Wickham 1995: 113).

At the London meeting of Preparatory Committee in 1946, the delegate from China raised the question to the US delegate about the meaning of the language used in paragraph 3 of Article 71 that NGO might undertake *'specific tasks'* for the ITO. US replied "while no formal delegation of power was intended, it was recognized that NGOs had 'research staffs' and 'facilities' that might be of use to the ITO, and that it might therefore be 'of value to the organization' to ask NGOs to carry out 'certain studies' (UN Doc E/PC/T/C.V/PV/2, 1946: 30). No further discussion was held regarding Article 71 paragraph 3. It was recommended by the report of the First Session of the Preparatory Committee that the paragraph was approved in its actual form and it was generally recognized that International Non-Governmental Organizations (INGOs) might play a helpful role.

However, in the Second Session of the Preparatory Committee of the UN Conference on Trade and Employment held in Geneva from April to October 1947; Article 71 paragraph 3 was modified. Rules of procedure were again amended to allow NGOs to consult with sub-groups of the Preparatory Committee. The scope of the participation of NGOs had widened as the Committee edited the reference to the four NGOs named during the first session (Sen 1994: 2803). So the rule at Geneva provides that "NGOs in Category 'A' of the Report of the *Committee of the Economic and Social Council on Arrangements for Consultation with Non-Governmental Organizations* should be permitted 'either directly or through committees established for the purpose', to consult with committees of the Preparatory Committee" (ICITO /EC.2/11, 1948: 4).

According to the ECOSOC Report (UN ECOSOC Resolution 1296 {XLIV}),

> Category 'A' includes those organization concerning with most of the activities of the Economic and Social Council and are associated with economic and social life of the

people. These NGOs have a consultative status in it. Typical organizations in Category A include those representing labour, management, business, farmers and consumers (p.4).

Despite the provisions under Article 71 paragraph 3, a small number of NGOs participated in the Geneva meeting because there was a lack of procedure for responding to the points being made by NGOs. US further proposed that the phrase in paragraph 3 *'may invite them to undertake specific tasks'* should be deleted as the first part of the paragraph had already addressed this; hence, there was no requirement of this clause. This change was accepted by the second session. Following this second session, the *UN Conference on Trade and Employment* finally met in Cuba, Havana from November 1947 to March 1948, which drew up the Havana Charter for the ITO to be submitted to the governments represented. The Article entitled *'Relations with Other Organizations'* (Article 71) was approved without any discussion. Due to the addition of new articles, the numbering of provisions changed. So that, Article 71 became Article 87 and the paragraph dealing with NGOs became paragraph 2 of the final Havana Charter for the ITO and Article 87(2) stipulated that "the organization may make suitable arrangements for consultation and cooperation with non-governmental organizations concerned with matters within the scope of this Charter" (ITO 1949: 353).

So, the NGO-related provision of the ITO Charter went beyond the UN Charter by adding 'cooperation' to 'consultation'. It is important to note that NGOs performed an essential role in the UN Havana conference. Organizations such as the *ICC, the ICA* and the *International Organization of Industrial Employers*, participated effectively in debate. It was decided that "papers submitted by NGOs would be circulated as Conference documents, and that the views of NGOs could be sponsored by any delegation" (UN Doc. Press Release/ITO/109, 6 December 1947);[3] and besides this, ITO might ask NGOs to go through any project analysis or to make suggestions to the organization on matters within their competence (E/CONF.2/15). It is significant that NGOs participated in both the Session of the Preparatory Committee as well as in the final UN Conference. NGOs having consultative status got recognition in the first session of the Preparatory Committee; whereas, during the UN Conferences in 1948, NGOs made broad policy statements for the consideration by the Committee. Hence, NGOs played an influential and substantial role in the deliberations that would lead to the creation of the ITO. This makes it

---

[3] Cited in Charnovitz and Wickham (1995): 115

clear that the provision [Article 87(2)] of the ITO Charter was approved among those who drafted the Charter without more argument over it (Charnovitz and Wickham 1995: 116).

Implementation of Article 87 Paragraph 2

In order to assess the utility and worth of Article 87(2), there is need to see how this provision was implemented. During the Havana Conference, government delegates adopted a resolution to establish an interim commission in place of the Preparatory Committee. Therefore, an *Interim Commission for the International Trade Organization (ICITO)* was set up to prepare the final agenda for the establishment of the ITO. This Commission had several functions, including to "prepare, in consultation with non-governmental organizations, for presentation to the first regular session of the Conference, recommendations regarding the implementation of the provisions of paragraph 2 of Article 87 of the Charter" (ITO 1949: 354).

The ICITO elected an Executive Committee of eighteen member countries to exercise its functions and nearly half of these were developing countries. This Executive Committee took over the functions of the ICITO. The Executive Committee met in August 1948 in Geneva and six NGOs attended this meeting – *ICC, ICA, the International Federation of Agricultural Producers, the International Organization of Industrial Employers, the Inter-Parliamentary Union,* and the *World Federation of United Nations Associations.* Among these groups, *ICC* asked to submit its views on ITO-NGO relations (ITO 1949: 542). It is relevant to note that ICC is one NGO that heavily supported trade liberalization and rights of foreign investors and has been active in this field for a long period of time (Sornarajah 2004: 269). The Committee specifically invited NGOs for the discussions over the ITO-NGO relations. Committee was assisted by the Secretariat and its Executive Secretary was Eric Wyndham White. This ICITO Secretariat was later on transformed into the GATT Secretariat.

After conducting discussions over the prospects of the implementation of Article 87, the Secretariat of the Interim Commission prepared a note entitled *"Relations with Non-Governmental Organizations"*, which served as the basis for recommendations. The Secretariat also reviewed practices of NGO involvement in other international organizations; and finally made some key points that are as follows (Charnovitz and Wickham 1995: 117):

- ECOSOC categorized NGOs based on their aim and scope of work and such categorization is too rigid and cannot apply in the field of international trade. So, it was recommended that the ITO shall adopt more flexible arrangements to cover a larger number of NGOs (national and international) having specialization on those issues directly related to the ITO's working agenda.

- NGOs may participate as observers in ITO Conferences and may have a right to submit their suggestions.

- "A list and brief description of all communications received from NGOs" should be circulated to ITO members by the ITO Director-General. "The Director-General should have the right to appoint advisory committees consisting of representatives of NGOs" (ICITO/EC.2/11, 1948: 6).

The Secretariat's note also provided a list of NGOs that would be involved in the ITO meeting. It included several organizations having interest in trade policy such as *ICC, ICA,* the *International Organization of Industrial Employers,* the *International Federation of Agricultural Producers,* the *International Association for the Protection of Industrial Property,* the *International Fairs Union,* the *World Federation of Trade Unions,* the *International Transport Workers Federation, and* the *International Federation of Christian Trade Unions.* It also included organizations having interest in social issues such as the *International Co-operative Women's Guild.* Few organizations submitted their proposal to the Secretariat; the ICC made many suggestions regarding the NGOs provision in the ITO Charter. The President of the ICC recommended that "it was important for ITO documents to reach it about three months in advance of ITO meetings to allow time for distribution and consultation" (ITO 1952: 648). NGOs' great desire to have interaction with ITO was also expressed when they said that they would always be ready to assist the ITO in its working culture.

Apart from that, various delegates also raised some important points. The delegate from Czechoslovakia noted that "ITO would be considering some highly confidential matters and therefore NGO relationship would have to be treated with the greatest care" (ICITO/EC.2/SR.8 1948: 4). The delegate from France expressed doubts over whether the constitution of the advisory committee was satisfactory. At the end of the discussion, the Executive Committee referred the matter of NGOs to the Subcommittee on Administration that followed Secretariat's notes (Ford 2002: 120).

The Report of the Subcommittee on Administration, headed by Mr. Tonkin, suggested that the ITO would make a list of organizations chosen from the ECOSOC list of organizations having consultative status in it. Besides this, the Committee could also add some more NGOs having special competence in the field of the ITO after consulting with the ECOSOC. The Subcommittee felt that NGOs could have a comfortable interaction with ITO outside the Conference also (ICITO/EC.2/21). In this respect, the delegate from Philippines stated that it is clear after a lot of discussion that the 'ITO would not be prevented from excluding NGOs from attending specific meetings when it so decided' (ICITO/EC.2/SR.13). In March 1949, the Secretariat of ICITO incorporated both discussions of the Executive Committee and contents of the Subcommittee's report into a draft of a Proposed Report of the Interim Commission. The draft of a Proposed Report of the Interim Commission to the First Conference of the ITO finally stated that "The organization shall take full advantage of the knowledge and experience of non-governmental organizations engaged in work within its purview. To this end, arrangements shall be made for including appropriate non-governmental organizations in a list of consultants to the organization" (Charnovitz and Wickham 1995: 120). This showed that the ITO empowered NGOs to attend conferences and to submit recommendations to the conference for consideration (Brandstetter 2003: 7).

Moreover, NGOs were to be able to receive any documentation necessary for effective consultation. However, the above-mentioned proposed report was never adopted as the ITO never came into existence due to the opposition by a few state members (E/CONF.2/BUR/13). Had opposition to the ITO not developed, provisions regarding ITO-NGO relations would be accepted by the First Conference of the ITO. The Proposed Report of the Interim Commission clearly demonstrates the intention of the founders of the trading system that there is coherence between NGOs and international trading system in terms of their aims and aspirations (Charnovitz 1996: 332).

Since negotiators failed to create any consensus over the formation of the ITO, they began parallel negotiations for the establishment of the GATT as multilateral trade negotiating forum in order to introduce tariffs reductions. The plan among negotiators called for the ITO to take control over the GATT, once the ITO was finalized. Since, the US failed to implement the ITO, the GATT was the only forum left. Negotiators had a plan to establish the ITO as a formal organization that was not implemented; therefore, they decided to set up a less formal trade agreement i.e. the GATT in order to resurrect the ITO Charter. On 1 January 1948, the GATT was signed by 23 countries including India. However, Chapter IV of the Havana Charter, which came into force in 1948 as the GATT, contained no provisions for the role of NGOs in its activities. It is to be noted that the ICITO remained in existence throughout the history of the GATT as the institutional embodiment of the GATT Agreement and was not terminated until late 1994 (Brandstetter 2003: 8).

While NGOs were not engaged in the working process of the GATT, they were active outside the forum in the field of international trade. During the 1950s and 1960s, NGOs in developed countries started working towards international cooperation in the field of trade (Meyer 1999: 6). For example, in the UK, in the late 1950s, *Oxfam* started an aid project entitled 'helping by selling' to support people who lived in developing countries. In this project, NGOs from developed countries bought products made in developing countries and then they sold them to consumers in developed countries. The main purpose was aid international cooperation. On the other hand, in the 1960s, many countries in Africa became independent and UNCTAD adopted a new slogan – "trade, not aid" – in order to encourage developing countries and LDCs to become financially independent from western countries (Brown 1993: 221).

GATT held eight rounds of multilateral trade negotiations from 1948 to 1994, among which the Tokyo and Uruguay Rounds are important from the context of the role of NGOs in international trade matters. The Tokyo Round was the seventh round of multilateral trade negotiation under the auspices of the GATT. One hundred and two countries participated in this Round, which began in 1973 and ended in 1979. This was the first trade round to deal with non-tariff barriers, which divided into different codes such as 'custom valuation, standards and government procurement' etc. (McRae and Thomas 1983: 52).

The Tokyo Round initiated the process of trade reform as the surrounding environment of the international trading system was starting to change. The US initiated this round after the 1971 economic crisis[4]. Since, it began in the midst of the oil crisis, deep recession, and consequently rising protectionism, it did not take place in a favourable economic and political environment (Spero and Hart 2009: 96). Issue of public participation in the GATT was first raised by the US during Tokyo Round. The US objective in the Tokyo Round was the adoption of fair labour standards and of right to petition by non-members in the GATT including non-governmental entities, transnational enterprises and academicians. That objective was never achieved because of the emergence of a new phase of protectionism (Charnovitz 1996: 332). That is why the Round did not pay attention to public participation in international trade. Although the Tokyo Round was an important step, it was the one that proved inadequate to move out protectionist pressure (Carty 1989: 707).

1980 onwards, the trading system had been transformed by the forces of globalization, which increased international trade and greater interdependence dramatically. Furthermore, the nature of trade was transformed by the increased trade in new fields like services, intellectual property and new investments in high technology industries. This created conflicting political demands by two different groups of actors. The first group comprised developed countries, transnational corporations and business interest groups, which called for the expansion of trade liberalization and global management of old and new trade issues. The second group including developing and least developed countries, non-governmental organizations demanded protection and a halt to the forces of globalization. Growing globalization put pressure on the GATT system. The precarious nature of the multilateral trading system was revealed in 1982, when the GATT held its ministerial meeting. The agenda of this meeting was ambitious which included new issues such as agriculture, trade in high technology and services etc (Meyer 1999: 12).

In the ensuing time, the Reagan administration of the US supported by the Prime Minister of the Japan and the GATT Secretariat began a campaign to launch a new round of multilateral trade negotiations. In 1985, world trade officials established a Committee to develop an agenda and in September 1986, a special session of the GATT contracting parties officially launched the negotiations, which came to be known as the Uruguay Round (1986-1994). Conflict started in the Uruguay Round with the beginning of the discussion on the inclusion of new trade related issues like services, IPR, agriculture subsidies and investment (Spero and Hart 2009: 103).

---

[4] The economic crisis of 1971 was primarily a crisis of overproduction, a crisis caused by decrease in profits. The markets in the developed world had gradually become too small for the multinational corporations.

Hence, while the Tokyo Round was a response to the protectionist measures adopted by countries in the field of trade; the Uruguay Round was a response to new developments in the world economy.

Developing countries became attentive towards the Uruguay Round because it provided them with an opportunity to express their grievances about western dominance over the market and the misuse of tariff and non-tariff barriers to the goods of developing countries (Wilkinson 1996: 251). This Round also provided a chance to argue against the increasing power of MNCs and their exploitation of natural and human resources (Moore 2003: 188).

During the late 1980s and early 1990s; international trade agenda was influenced by the GATT Uruguay Round negotiations. This Round was going to include new non-traditional areas, which might affect the public interest, health, human rights, natural resources and environment. Accordingly, NGOs concerns began to focus on Uruguay Round's potentially devastating effect on the above discussed areas and interests of developing world. For this, NGOs tended to target their national delegations and ministries participating in the Uruguay Round as well as the ongoing negotiation process of the Round because NGOs did not have a direct involvement in the Uruguay Round of negotiation process (Ford 2002: 118). For instance, *International Coalition for Development Action (ICDA)* formed in 1975 in order to provide a framework for effective lobbying campaigns on development issues. During the Uruguay Round, NGOs campaign focused on the need for structural changes in international trade and finances according to the idea of sustainable economic development, public interests and welfare (Wilkinson 1996: 255).

The NGO-GATT Steering Committee

In December 1988, state representatives met again in Montreal, Canada to assess the progress made in the Round and to clarify the agenda for the remaining years. This GATT ministerial mid-term review meeting was met by thousands of anti-globalization protesters. This is one of the first organized civil society challenges to the GATT and later the WTO. Moreover, an NGO *"Shadow GATT Conference"* was held in Montreal. In 1987, *Institute for Agriculture and Trade Policy (IATP)* began to organize and report on the launched Uruguay Round because issues to be discussed in the Round would have an influence over the national agricultural policies around the globe. IATP was the only American NGO present when the GATT negotiating forum agreed for the creation of the WTO in Marrakech in 1994. IATP organized the GATT Workshop for farm leaders, agricultural policy makers and other NGOs in Geneva (Ford 2002: 124).

The following year (in 1989), an UNCTAD NGO Forum met in Geneva to trace the GATT talks. At this forum, the NGO-GATT Steering Committee was established that comprised of development and environmental NGOs from developed as well as developing countries, for example, *OXFAM, Christian Aid* and *TWN* etc. Myriam Vander Stichele, the chief negotiator/ trade program coordinator for *ICDA*, took over the general administration duties of the Steering Committee. Simon Stocker, Director of *EUROSTEP(European Solidarity Towards Equal Participation of People)*, and Clive Robinson of *Christian Aid* were co-chairs. Here, it is interesting to note that the majority were European NGOs focussing on trade and development issues because during the course of the Uruguay Round, network of European NGOs played an important role and a number of associations of European development NGOs were mobilized such as the *Association of Protestant Development Organizations in Europe (APRODEV), the International Cooperation for Development and Solidarity Europe (EURO-CIDSE); and EUROSTEP*. These NGOs were active in the Steering Committee (Lang 2011: 69). The Steering Committee became effective in coordinating different activities and conferences of NGOs to facilitate lobbying on common positions to put pressure over the Uruguay Round. They sent the position papers to the respective contracting parties and national delegations of the GATT (Wilkinson 1996: 252).

When the GATT Ministerial Conference met in Brussels in December of 1990, a group of NGOs did protest across the Conference area and denounced the ongoing round as a *GATTastrophe* (Charnovitz 2000: 175). NGO groups delivered unsolicited briefs to the GATT Secretariat for consideration. However, these briefs were never considered as the GATT Secretariat argued that it was an inter-governmental system. An open forum by *ICDA* was organized, which came to be known as Shadow Conference from November to December 1990. It was attended by twenty eight NGOs from the North and twenty seven from the South. The forum was funded by a dozen of the larger NGOs. It made a 10-point declaration entitled '*A People's GATT for World Development'* together with a document entitled '*Bringing GATT Out of the Shadows'*. This served as a lobbying instrument for the *'GATTastrophe'*. This forum included members from environmental, consumers', farmers', and church and development organizations (Brandstetter 2003: 9).

Several NGO groups organized seminars, for example, *Research Group for an Alternative Economic Strategy (GRESEA)* is a Brussels based research centre with NGO status, founded in 1978 by members of trade unions, development NGOs, the academic community and international organizations. It organized several public discussions and seminars on the GATT negotiations, which included *'Issues Left Out by the Uruguay Round: Environment, Social Rights and Democracy'* (Wilkinson 1996: 254).

In 1992, *IATP, American Federation of Labour and Congress of Industrial Organizations (AFL-CIO), Friends of the Earth, National Farmers Union, Public Citizen* and *the Sierra Club* joined hands in organizing *Trade for the 21st Century* in Washington DC. The UN Conference on Environment and Development known as Earth Summit met in Rio de Janeiro and the IATP co-hosted the Global Forum on the GATT at the summit. IATP published the legal critique of the GATT Tuna-Dolphin decision, which ruled against of the US legislation aimed to save dolphins from injury to the nets of Tuna fishermen. Thus, it has been observed that NGOs' activities were wide and varied throughout the period of the Uruguay Round. Apart from that, much work was undertaken by individual NGO also. For instance, *Third World Network (TWN)* organized a meeting in Penang, in response to the introduction of new issues in the Uruguay Round, because of which it was seen as 'trimming the nation-state'. During the Uruguay Round of GATT talks in the early 1990s, TWN was one of the groups of civil society organizations which strongly opposed the Multilateral Trade Negotiations by calling it 'undemocratic' and 'non-transparent' (Brown 2003: 76).

By the end of 1992, NGOs addressed the proposed post-GATT system of rules. On November 1992, *ICDA* with other NGOs like *Germanwatch,* organized an *International NGO Conference on the Multilateral Trading Organization* in Hamburg. This Conference made a common declaration entitled *'The US-EC Talks on the Uruguay Round: Developing Countries suffer from the Democratic Deficit'*. After few days, it also organized another conference on *trade and people* in Brussels. Groups of NGOs organized many conferences to oppose the negotiation process of the Uruguay Round because GATT failed to take into consideration the interests of the Third World (Wilkinson 1996: 254). Regarding this, in 1992, Dianna Melrose, public policy director of the *OXFAM* stated "our call was that the European Community should show real leadership in GATT in trying to promote the interests of developing countries" (Allen 1997: 330).

In addition to that, NGOs called for the trade negotiations to be made more democratic, accountable and transparent, for which they proposed to make the advisory councils include members from amongst rural-urban workers, consumers, women, small producers, human rights activists, indigenous and minority people and environmentalist and other NGOs (Lang 2011: 70).

Responses of NGOs on new themes

- **Trade Related Aspects of Intellectual Property Rights (TRIPS):** NGOs expressed their concern over the issue of inclusion of new themes such as IPRs in the trade agenda during the Uruguay Round. "Northern NGOs felt that any GATT rules should be limited to trade distortions such as counterfeit goods, that any extension of IPRs to life forms would reduce genetic diversity and threaten food security and must be prohibited" (Vivekanandan and Giri 2001: 139). The TRIPS agreement would require countries to accept conventions and allow the use of multilateral trading organization's enforcement mechanism. This would increase the revenue of industrialized countries as developing countries are net importers of technology in the field of IPR (Brown 2003: 76). On 5th April, 1994, huge number of demonstrators marched through New Delhi amid violent clashes with police in protest over the effects of the implementation of TRIPS Agreement on India's agrarian economy. In particular, they were outraged because the new trade rules would give power to multinational seed merchants and enable them to enforce copyright on scientifically improved seeds. Southern NGOs raised questions about national sovereignty for instance, under the India Patent Act 1970, inventions relating to agricultural and horticultural processes were not patentable. However, the GATT now obliged India to make their national laws in the line of IPR rules under TRIPS Agreement (Matthews 2002: 8).

- **Trade Related Investment Measures (TRIMs):** On trade related investment measures, NGOs declared that the people of developing countries should hold and protect their rights to develop their own service and manufacturing sectors in accordance with their development objectives. They should also keep their rights to regulate investment and the behaviour of TNCs. Since TRIMs prohibits the use of investment measures by national governments for their national interests, it would accord all rights to foreign investors with no obligations in return. *TWN* argued that UNCTAD, not the WTO is the appropriate forum for comprehensive discussion on the investment measures and development process (Brown 2003: 77).

While NGOs' campaign had an influential impact on the *Uruguay Round of Trade Negotiations*, this could be considered as modest success only. "The *Catholic Institute for International Relations (CIIR)* study found that NGOs' approaches to the broader issues of international trade suffered from poor information, lack of credibility with the target audience, poor public support and few tangible campaigning points" (Wilkinson 1996: 260). Hence, this had limited NGOs' overwhelming effect on the GATT negotiation process.

It has been observed that non-governmental groups took all efforts (lobbying and campaigning) outside the forum of the Uruguay Round and did not get any direct representation and participation in the negotiation process of the GATT Round. However, efforts regarding the participation and consultation with NGOs were to be taken under consideration by the negotiating groups of the GATT. Due to the working on several issues, GATT discussion panel was divided into different issue based negotiating groups and committees, for example, *Committee on Technical Barriers to Trade* and *Negotiating Group on Basic Telecommunications.*

During Uruguay Round, discussion over the formation of panels in the Dispute Settlement Body was also held in order to assist parties to the dispute while making decisions. In this respect, paragraph 1 and 2 of the section of the 1984 Decision on "Formation of Panels" provide that (L/5718/Rev.1)

> "Contracting Parties should indicate to the Director-General the names of persons they think qualified to serve as panellists who are not presently affiliated with national administrations but who have a higher degree of knowledge of international trade and experience of the GATT and that these names should be used to develop a roster of non-

governmental panellists to be agreed upon by the Contracting Parties in consultations with the Director- General".

Again,

"In the event that panel composition cannot be agreed within thirty days after a matter is referred by the Contracting Parties, the Director-General shall, at the request of either party and in consultation with the Chairman of the Council, complete the panel by appointing persons from the roster of non-governmental panellists to resolve the deadlock, after consulting both parties".

Although a preparatory list of panellists was made by Contracting Parties, it was extended and reproduced with time (in 1986, 1989, 1990 and 1994) and not finalized until the conclusion of the Uruguay Round. At the meeting in 1990, the parties made a roster of non-governmental panellists with some additional nominations, which included academicians, former parliamentarians and trade representatives; and also non-governmental organizations. In comparison with other panellists, it showed the inclusion of less number of NGOs per se, for example, *Bangladesh Institute for Development Studies,* and *Institute for Research on Public Policy (Geneva), Institute for International Economic Affairs (Japan);* and *National Association of Manufacturers (USA)* (L/6763). This roster of non-governmental panellists was not taken into consideration by the GATT council. Hence, while the issue of participation of non-governmental entities was to be discussed among negotiators during Uruguay Round; they had failed to address the issue adequately due to the lack of consensus among them.

In 1994, a *Preparatory Committee for the World Trade Organization* was established to conclude and implement the final act of the Uruguay Round that had the task of founding an inter-governmental organization i.e. WTO and to ensure its efficient operation. P. D. Sutherland was appointed as the Chairman of the Committee. Committee was open for membership to all signatories of the final act and it was divided into sub-committees. It was serviced by the GATT Secretariat and decisions were to be made by consensus (PC/R/W1/Rev.2).

With respect to the participation of observers in the Uruguay Round negotiations, no observer status had been granted to any non-governmental organizations. Regional and inter-governmental organizations were invited to participate as observers in the meeting. Since Sub-

Committees and negotiating groups on different issues could invite any organization to attend formal meeting as observers, they usually invited the regional and inter-governmental organizations. For instance, the Negotiating Group on Basic Telecommunications had granted observer status to UNCTAD and the *International Telecommunication Union (ITU)*. Negotiating Group on TRIMS invited the World Bank and the IMF as observers. Moreover, in the Preparatory Committee, there was no participation of non-governmental groups, not even of business interest groups, for example, ICC requested the Sub-Committee on Services for participation as observer status, which was not considered by the Sub-Committee. However, this Sub-Committee had granted observer status to the World Bank, IMF, UN and the UNCTAD (PC/SCS/W/5).

The question of the participation of organizations was also raised in the context of the preparations for the Marrakesh Ministerial meeting. Representatives of various NGOs attended the Uruguay Round signatory meeting in Marrakesh in 1994 and presented alternative public briefings, however, they were admitted to the meeting as 'Press' (Charnovitz and Wickham 1995: 118). Thus, NGOs criticized the elitism and secrecy of the meeting.

Throughout the *Uruguay Round of Trade Negotiations*, environmental NGOs, unlike other development NGOs, have had an influential impact on the negotiation process, which led the GATT Contracting Parties to create a Committee on Trade and Environment. A Public Symposium on Trade, Environment and Sustainable Development was hosted by the GATT Secretariat held in Geneva on 10 and 11 June of 1994. The two principle objectives of the symposium were to provide information about the work being done by the GATT on trade and environment; and to bring together recognized experts on related fields to examine and debate the role that trade policies can play in environmental protection and conservation and vice-versa. This is to say that the symposium would represent the start of a process of dialogue between NGOs, the GATT Secretariat and delegations (TE 008).

Outside the trading system, several foundations, institutes and NGOs evaluated the GATT's standard of rules and began working to increase its openness. "A handbook sponsored by the *Environmental Grantmakers Association* and the *Consultative Group on Biological Diversity* pointed out that GATT deliberations remained closed to citizen input and involvement and noted the contrast with UN agencies that were open to such input" (Charnovitz 2000: 177).

In 1993-94, a group of experts drafted the *Winnipeg Principles on Trade and Sustainable Development*. One of those principles was that GATT Panels should entertain written submissions from non-governmental actors. According to some analysts, trade negotiations could be democratized only by granting observer status to NGOs (IISD 1995: 18). When the process of approving the Uruguay Round Trade Negotiations began in 1994, US Congress readdressed the issue of the closed nature of the GATT and dispute settlement mechanism after the Tokyo Round (Mason 2003: 24). In a speech on Capitol Hill, US Trade Representative Mickey Kantor characterized the GATT panel process as "Star Chamber proceedings that are making the most important decisions that affect the lives of all of our citizens – especially in the environmental area – and there is no accountability whatsoever" (Charnovitz 2000: 178). The US Congress sought the adoption of those procedures in the final act of the Uruguay Round that would ensure transparency in trade matters by the multilateral trade organization.

1990 onwards, pressures from globalization and liberalization led to an increase in international trade and consequently the emergence of new issues and disputes in various fields like labour and environment. High profile disputes such as the *tuna–dolphin* and the *shrimp-turtle* cases attracted the attention of several NGOs. Thus, the increased interest and interaction of NGOs in the international trading system is co-terminus with the expansion of its mandate in the Marrakesh Ministerial meeting (Sampson 2001: 161). The Final Act concluding the Uruguay Round and officially establishing the WTO regime was signed during the April 1994 ministerial meeting at Marrakesh; and the draft text for the international trading system also included the provision regarding the NGOs participation under the Article V.2 of the Marrakesh Agreement. Article V.2 of the WTO provided that "the General Council may make appropriate arrangements for consultation and cooperation with NGOs concerned with matters related to those of the WTO". However, WTO General Council took eighteen months to implement the NGO provision in the *Agreement on Establishing the World Trade Organization*. WTO Article V.2 is essentially the same provision as was agreed to at the ITO Preparatory Conference of 1946 (Charnovitz and Wickham 1995: 122).

The WTO as successor of the GATT modified the international trading system by increasing free trade across globe, expanding trade agenda and membership. Unlike the GATT, the WTO brought significant improvements in its organizational structure such as Dispute

Settlement Body and enforcement mechanisms. Apart from the Article V (2) of the WTO Agreement, 1996 Guidelines was also introduced in order to promote WTO-NGO relationship. Currently NGOs interact with the WTO members through various means such as public symposia, seminar, workshop and plenary meetings of the Ministerial Conference; and informal meetings etc. Beside this, NGOs may also influence the WTO members by submitting *amicus curiae* brief to the WTO Panel. This shows increased participation of NGOs in the WTO.

During Ministerial Conferences, NGOs presented either confrontational or co-operational approach. While Seattle conference in 1999 showed NGOs opposition to the WTO policies; Hong Kong (2005) and Geneva Conference (2009) expressed cooperative interaction between NGO and WTO members. Unlike business groups, development and environmental NGOs opposed the WTO agenda and introduction of Singapore issues[5] that would harm the interests of people of developing countries and LDCs; and also our ecological system. For instance, IATP, Action Aid and Oxfam presented their analytical review of the impact of trade liberalization on the agriculture and food security. According to NGOs, there is a lack of regulation for food security in the WTO. However, some NGOs such as Consumers for World Trade, Washington Council on International Trade and ICC support WTO's free trade policies because removing trade barriers would promote economic growth worldwide including developing countries and LDCs.

Seattle Ministerial Conference was held to launch a new round of trade negotiations following Uruguay Round. Nevertheless, NGOs demonstration at large scale led to the collapse of Seattle talks. This had restricted the NGOs participation in the next Doha Ministerial Conference in 2001, which then successfully launched new trade round i.e. Doha Development Round.

Doha Round is the current trade negotiation round of the WTO which is likely to affect the following areas: agriculture, services, relationship between trade and environment, WTO subsidies and the relationship between IPR and public health, the protection of biological diversity and traditional knowledge etc. Implementation of the Doha Round will facilitate the global trade and economic interdependence between countries. This Round is opposed not only

---

[5] Issues: Trade and investment, trade and competition policy, government procurement and trade facilitation.

by the NGO sector but also by a group of developing countries and LDCs as this agenda will negatively affect the interests of their people (WT/MIN (01)/ DEC/1). NGOs' confrontational approach towards the Doha Development Agenda indicates the uprising of anti-free trade movement at global level. Consequently, differences on issues such as agriculture subsidies between developed and developing countries and NGOs opposition create barriers in the successful implementation of the Doha Agenda.

Hence 1990 onwards, increased interaction of NGOs with the international trading system has impacted the dynamics of trade negotiations and rule making agenda of states. The WTO continues to be a central target of NGOs in order to focus on the neoliberal trade policies and foster equitable economic growth and sustainable development. As the WTO is a member-based organization consisting of representatives largely from national trade ministries, the organization has not yet made any institutional mechanisms for a concrete participation of NGOs in the international trade negotiation process. This shows that international trading system still remains to be an inter-state system and NGOs are kept away from the main negotiating corridors of the multilateral trade organization.

Conclusion

Currently, thousands of NGOs are involved in the field of trade from local level to international level. INGOs and NGOs alliances work on several issues in the field of international trade such as agriculture, subsidies, anti-dumping and economic development for LDCs and developing countries (CONGO 2006: 4). Unlike trade unions and business groups, development and environmental NGOs are considered as modern players in the field of international trade as they started to increasingly involve in trade field with the increased significance of globalization and trade liberalization (Guay et.al. 2004: 128).

1990 onwards, the outgrowth of neo-liberalism in the field of world trade promoted the principle of 'trade without borders' i.e. free trade; therefore, NGOs began to build their business skills and knowledge and target the trade policy and markets. Since trade program address a wider range of development issues – from women to the environment and poor communities, this necessitates the involvement of NGOs in the trade related activities. However, NGOs role and activities depend on their approach towards trade, for instance, whether they are pro-trade or not.

Those NGOs that participate in the major pro-trade campaigns look at trade as a means of development and this includes not only business interest group like *ICC* and *Washington Council on International Trade* but also humanitarian and development organizations like *Care International*. Many of these consider that development and expansion of trade proves more effective in fighting poverty than humanitarian aid alone. Some NGOs such as human rights and environmental NGOs are against free trade as it harms the public interests and ecological balance. They campaign for fair trade rather free trade, generating a debate over 'free trade' versus 'fair trade'.

Free Trade vs. Fair Trade and NGOs Stand

Free trade can be defined as a policy through which nations do trade (export-import) without applying tariffs and non-tariff barriers so that trading partners can achieve mutual gains from trade of goods and services. The main features of free trade policy are as follows: trade of goods and services without trade barriers such as quotas or subsidies, free access to markets, and free movement of labour and capital within/ between countries. Mostly NGOs such as *Consumers for World Trade (CWT), Washington International Trade Association* are pro-free trade NGOs and believe that reducing and eliminating trade barriers between nations leads to economic stability and prosperity and ensures a better quality of life for all people. *CWT* an American non-profit and non-partisan organization is a strong supporter of the *North America Free Trade Agreement (NAFTA)* and the *WTO*. Whereas, NGOs such as *Consumer Unity and Trust Society (CUTS), Fair Trade Watch, International Federation for Alternative Trade, Public Citizen's Global Trade Watch* are anti-free trade NGOs claiming that free trade rules work best for those who are already rich, resourceful and developed in high technology area. Thus, it increases the gap between the rich developed countries and developing/ least developed countries who are already struggling to compete (Chang 2003: 8).

Anti-free trade NGOs emphasize the alternative form of trade to overcome the problems regarding the free trade policy, which is known as 'Fair Trade'. This alternative form of trade is a system that underlines the importance of 'equal exchange' between developing countries and developed countries. In addition, fair trade supporters support trade that should be carried out directly between the consumer side and producer side to maintain transparency and equality (Smith and Barrientos 2005: 194).

Fair Trade Movement and Alternative Trade Organization in the era of Globalization

During the 1980s, with the emergence of the concept of 'sustainable development' and the slogan 'trade, not aid' by UNCTAD, fair trade movement has arisen. Earlier these fair trade groups started their activities as charity to save people from hunger or disasters in developing and least developed countries. Many groups have a religious background, for example, *OXFAM* as a Christian Group began their activities during the Second World War by raising money for poor people. However, they began to change gradually their form of activities after accepting the idea of fair trade as an alternative form of trade in order to enhance the economic independence of developing countries and LDCs. The fair trade movement proposes a fundamentally different market system that would be a challenge to the global capitalist system (Leclair 2002: 952).

As the process of globalization has accelerated, the shortcomings of the unrestrained free trade have been revealed, which are addressed by the non-governmental actors. Consequently, a significant number of Alternative Trade Organizations (ATO) have formed to implement and promote fair trade activity. "In the industrialized countries, organizations have been conducting their storefront operations by offering products from developing countries at subsidized prices such as *OXFAM, Bridgehead* (Canada) and *Nepali Bazaro* (Japan)" (Leclair 2002: 949). In developing countries, on the other hand, these organizations target not only producers of developing countries but also their services providing to a marginalized group such as refugee, women and disabled person etc. Although functions of these two forms of alternative trade are different, they both believe in equitable economic growth and welfare of every individual of the world (Bhagwati 1994: 234).

According to some observers, growth of an idea of alternative trade is strongly associated with the growth of NGOs and their increased influence. Organizations such as *Focus on the Global South*, the *'Our World is not for Sale' Network,* and *Global Exchange* and other civil society groups are consistent in their message that significant number of people could escape from poverty only with a fairer trading system. *OXFAM* in its 'Make Trade Fair' campaign notes that 'if Africa, East Asia and South Asia, and Latin America were each to increase their share of world exports of by one percent, the resulting gains in income could lift 128 million people out of poverty' (OXFAM 2002: 5). In 1989, *the International Federation for Alternative Trade (IFAT)* formed between dozens of organizations to create a global support network to promote fair trade from production to sale, which has now changed its name as *World Fair Trade Organization (WFTO)* (WFTO Annual Report 2009: 2).

The most comprehensive manifestation of fair trade can be seen as a part of the NGO movement. In contrast to larger official institutions such as the *World Bank* and the *IMF*, NGOs are able to target the needs of poor people as they have situation-specific programs and can maintain local linkages and they promote social and organizational development. If the inter-governmental organizations that drive trade policy are to increase the development impact of trade, they should bring NGOs into the mainstream of trade and development. Mostly, international institutions and their trade development efforts are limited to only the economic goals i.e. trade and business. NGOs experience in many sides of development can help to address these limitations. NGOs can broaden the trade development objectives of IGOs by including the environmental and social aspects of trade development. NGOs may assist in evaluation of new perspectives on how trade policy affects environment, health and other issues and vice-versa. NGOs can be partners in projects and ensure a participatory dialogue in project design. Large advocacy campaigns for trade development raise awareness and generate public support that could help to drive out the problems facing by IGOs regarding the implementation of trade policy. Hence, NGOs may be fruitful in construction and dissemination of knowledge about international trade (Murphy 2010: 24).

However, NGOs activities are mostly seen in the form of confrontation and protestation since the Battle in Seattle 1999, which restrict the inclusive involvement of NGOs in the international trading system. In practice, NGOs' role is more nuanced. A review of the historical record of NGOs shows that unlike the GATT/WTO, UN and its related bodies such as the UNCTAD and UNDP have been the most avid supporters and co-operators of NGOs both in their development and advocacy roles. Throughout its history, GATT somehow expressed apathy towards NGO participation in the trade negotiation process as states were struggling for their economic development goals and world peace and security and there was lack of consensus among member states about the utility aspect of NGOs. Post Second World War period, NGOs seeking to represent social and environment concerns had less propitious conditions to affect the policy outcome of international trade negotiation process; therefore NGOs had a limited role in the field of international trade.

1990 onwards, the rising phenomena of trade liberalization and establishment of the WTO as the successor of the GATT expanded the trade agenda by including new areas such as IPR, services, agriculture and investment that had social and environmental impact. NGOs growing in number and scope at international level began to pay attention towards the WTO agenda. This period of globalization and evolution of Information and Communication Technology (ICT) created a comfortable space for NGOs to spread themselves across the globe as transnational advocacy networks. This also marked the significance of NGOs as efficient delivery mechanism and holders of expertise and knowledge at the international level. It prompted IGOs such as the WTO to have some informal provisions in its constitution regarding the role of NGOs. Consequently, the WTO Agreement established some laws related to NGO participation in the organization that generated a new controversial debate and thereby a need to address and discover roles and tactics employed by NGOs in the international trade governance i.e. the WTO.

Bibliography

Allen, Chris (1997), "Who Needs Civil Society?" *Review of African Political Economy,* 24(73), 329-37.

Arrangements between the GATT and Uruguay Round Bodies and International Organizations (1994), Sub-Committee on Institutional, Procedural and Legal Matters, Preparatory Committee for the WTO, GATT Doc. PC/IPL/W/3, 15 July.

Bhagwati, Jagdish (1994), "Free Trade: Old and New Challenges", *The Economic Journal,* 104(423), March, 231-246.

Blackett, Adelle (2007), *Trade Liberalization, Labour Law and Development: A Contextualization,* Geneva: International Institute for Labour Studies.

Blagescu, Monica and Young, John (2005), *Partnerships and Accountability: Current Thinking and Approaches among Agencies Supporting Civil Society Organizations,* Working Paper 255, August, UK: Overseas Development Institute.

Brown, Graham K. (2003), "Stemming the Tide: Third World Network and Global Governance", in Olav Schram Stokke and Oystein B. Thommessen (eds.), *Yearbook of International Cooperation on Environment and Development 2003-2004,* London: Earthscan Publications, 73-77.

Brown, Michael Barratt (1993), *Fair Trade: Reform and Realities in the International Trading System,* London and New Jersey: Zed Books.

Buechler, Steven M. (1995), "New Social Movement Theories", *The Sociological Quarterly,* 36(3), 441-64.

Carty, Anthony (1989), "International Trade and the Tokyo Round Negotiation by G. R. Winham: Reviewed Work", *The International and Comparative Law Quarterly,* 38(3), July, 707-09.

Chang, Ha-Joon (2001), "Breaking the Mould: An Institutionalist Political Economy Alternative to the Neoliberal Theory of the Market and the State", *Social Policy and Development Program Paper- United Nations Research Institute for Social Development (UNRISD),* Paper Number 6, May 2001, 1-34, [Online: web] Accessed 28 October 2009 URL:http://www.unrisd.org/80256B3C005BCCF9/(httpPublications)/44552A491D461D018025 6B5E003CAFCC?OpenDocument

Chang, Ha-Joon (2003), "Kicking Away the Ladder: The 'Real' History of Free Trade", A Paper Presented at the Conference on "Globalization and the Myth of Free Trade", 18 April 2003, [Online: web] Accessed 14 October 2009 URL: http://74.125.153.132/search?q=cache:zTOSsTaY608J:www.newschool.edu/cepa/originalsite/pa pers/workshop/chang_030419.doc.

Charnovitz, Steve (1996), "Participation of Non-Governmental Organizations in the World Trade Organizations", *Journal of International Economic Law,* 17(1), 331-357.

Charnovitz, Steve (1998), "The Moral Exception in Trade Policy", *Virginia Journal of International Law,* 38, [Online: web] Accessed 14 November 2009 URL: http://www.worldtradelaw.net/articles/charnovitzmoral.pdf

Charnovitz, Steve and Wickham, John (1995), "Non-Governmental Organizations and the Original International Trade Regime", *Journal of World Trade,* 29(5): 111-22.

Committee on Technical Barriers to Trade (1989), General Agreement on Tariffs and Trade (GATT), TBT/M/3, 21 December.

Consortium for Trade and Development (CENTAD) (2009), "Trade and Public Health", *Trading Up- Trade and Development Quarterly,* V (1), 1-32.

Consultative Relationship between the United Nations and Non-Governmental Organizations, UN Doc. ECOSOC Resolution 1996/31, Article 71, UN Charter.

Curtis, John M., "Involving NGOs in Trade Policy Negotiations", *The Journal of Public Management,* Optimum, 30(2), 60-62.

Deborah Eade and Alan Leather (eds.) (2004), 'Trade Union and NGO Relations in Development and Social Justice', *Development in Practice,* 14(1-2), 5-285.

Deese, David A (2008), *World Trade Politics: Power, Principles and Leadership*, USA: Routledge.

Domoto, Akiko, "International Environmental Governance- Its Impact on Social and Human Development", in Ginkel, Hans Van (eds.) (2002), *Human Development and the Environment: Challenges for the United Nations in the New Millennium,* Tokyo: UNU Press.

Draft of Agreements between the International Trade Organization and Other International Trade Organs (1948), Interim Commission, ICITO/EC.2/2, 14 October.

Dymond, William A.(2001), "Core Labour Standards and The World Trade Organization: Labour's Love Lost", *Canadian Foreign Policy,* 8(3), 99-114.

Esty, Daniel C.(1994), *Greening the GATT: Trade, Environment, and the Future*, Washington DC: Institute for International Economics.

Esty, Daniel C. (2001), "Bridging the Trade-Environment Divide", *Journal of Economic Perspectives,* 15(3): 113-30.

Fee, Elizabeth and Korstad, Robert R. (1991), "Public Health Then and Now: Understanding History to Shape the Future- The New Editor's Vision", *American Journal of Public Health,* 81(6), June, 81(6), 781-82.

Ford, Jane (2002), "A Social Theory of Trade Regime Change: GATT to WTO", *International Studies Review,* 4(3), 115-38.

General Committee Participation of Non-Governmental Organizations in the Work of the Conference (1947), UN Conference on Trade and Employment, UN Doc. E/CONF.2/BUR/13,15 December.

Grieco, Joseph M. (2000), "The International Political Economy since World War II", Columbia International Affairs Online (CIAO) Curriculum Case Study Project, October,[Online: web] Accessed 24 November 2009 URL: http://docs.google.com/viewer?a=v&q=cache:rnYQAjaQ_uEJ:www.ciaonet.org/casestudy/grj01/grj01.pdf.

Guay, Terrence, Doh, Jonathan P. and Sinclair, Graham (2004), "Non-Governmental Organizations, Shareholder Activism, and Socially Responsible Investments: Ethical, Strategic, and Governance Implications", *Journal of Business Ethics,* 52(1), 125-39.

Hall, Peter A. (1989), *The Political Power of Economic Ideas: Keynesianism across Nations,* New Jersey: Princeton University Press.

International Centre for Trade and Sustainable Development (ICTSD) (1998), "Fifty Years Later: Public Participation in the Multilateral Trading System", *Bridges,* 2(4), June.

ICITO /EC.2/11 (1948) *Interim Commission of the International Trade Organization - Executive Committee - Second Session - Relations with Non-Governmental Organizations - Note by the Secretariat of the Interim Commission for the International Trade Organization - (Item 5 of Provisional Agenda),* 15 July.

ICITO/EC.2/SR.8/Corr.1 (1948), *Interim Commission of the International Trade Organization - Executive Committee - Second Session - Corrigendum to Summary Record of Eighth Meeting,* 6 September 1948.

ICITO/EC.2/SR.13 (1948), *Interim Commission of the International Trade Organization - Executive Committee - Second Session - Summary Record of the Thirteenth Meeting - Held at the Palais des Nations, Geneva, on Tuesday, 14 September 1948, at 10 a.m.,* 17 September 1948.

ICITO/EC.2/21 (1948), *Interim Commission of the International Trade Organization - Executive Committee - Second Session - Drafts of A between the International Trade Organization and Other International Organs - Note by Executive Secretary,* 4 October 1948.

"International Trade Organization (Interim Commission)", *International Organization,* 3(2), May 1949, 353-54.

"International Trade Organization (Interim Commission)", *International Organization,* 3(3), August 1949, 542-43.

"International Trade Organization (ITO)", *International Organization,* 6(4), November 1952, 647-49.

Jackson, John H. (et.al) (1982), "Implementing the Tokyo Round: Legal Aspects of Changing International Economic Rules", *Michigan Law Review,* 81(2), December, 267-397, [Online: web] Accessed 30 January 2010 URL: http://www.jstor.org/stable/1288518

Jones, Kent (2004), *Who's Afraid of the WTO?* New York: Oxford University Press.

Leclair, Mark S. (2002), "Fighting the Tide: Alternative Trade Organizations in the Era of Global Free Trade", *World Development,* 30(6), 949-58.

Lenoszka, Anna (2003), "The Global Politics of Intellectual Property Rights and Pharmaceutical Drug Policies in Developing Countries", *International Political Science Review,* 24(2): 181-97.

Mason, Michael (2003), "The World Trade Regime and Non-Governmental Organizations: Addressing Trans national Environmental Concerns", [Online: web] Accessed 23 October 2009 URL: http://eprints.lse.ac.uk/571/

Marya, CM (2011), *A Textbook of Public Health Dentistry,* New Delhi: Jaypee Brothers Medical Publishers (P) Ltd.

Mathews, Jessica T. (1997), "Power Shift", *Foreign Affairs,* January/February, 76(1), 50-66.

Matthews, Duncan (2002), "Trade-Related Aspects of Intellectual Property Rights: Will the Uruguay Round Consensus Hold?" Centre for the Study of Globalization and Regionalization (CSGR) Working Paper No. 99/02, June [Online: web] Accessed 12 December 2009 URL: http://wrap.warwick.ac.uk/2019/

Mc Michael, A J and Beaglehole R (2000), "The Changing Global Context of Public Health", *Lancet,* 356(9228), August 5, 495-99 [Online: web] Accessed 14 January 2010 URL: http://www.ncbi.nlm.nih.gov/pubmed/10981904.

McRae, D. M. and Thomas, J. C. (1983), "The GATT and Multilateral Treaty Making: the Tokyo Round", *American Journal of International Law,* 77(1), January, 51-83 [Online: web] Accessed 30 January 2010 URL: http://www.jstor.org/stable/2201198

Meyer, Carrie A. (1999), "The Political Economy of NGOs and Globalization", [Online: web] Accessed 2 January 2010 URL: http://economics.gmu.edu/working/WPE_99/99_07.pdf

Mondal, Priyanka (2009), "The Legal Inter-Linkages: Trade, Environment and Development", *American Journal of Economics and Business Administration,* 1(3), 268-74, [Online: web] Accessed 14 January 2010 URL: http://www.scipub.org/fulltext/ajeba/ajeba13268-274.pdf

Moore, Mike (2003), *A World Without Walls: Freedom, Development, Free Trade and Global Governance,* UK: Cambridge University Press.

Murphy, Hanna (2010), *Making of International Trade Policy: NGOs, Agenda Setting and the WTO,* UK: Edward Elgar Publishing Ltd.

Negotiating Group on Dispute Settlement: Note by Secretariat (1987), Multilateral Trade Negotiations the Uruguay Round, GATT Doc. MTN.GNG/NG13/2, 15 July.

Oatley, Thomas H. (2001), "Multilateralizing Trade and Payments in Post-War Europe", *International Organizations,* 55(4), 949-69.

Oxfam International (2002), *Rigged Rules and Double Standards: Trade, Globalization and the Fight Against Poverty,* [Online: web] Accessed 22 February 2012 URL: http://www.maketradefair.com.

Participation of Observers: Note by the Secretariat (1994), Preparatory Committee for the World Trade Organization: Sub-Committee on Services, GATT Doc. PC/SCS/W/5, 15 September.

Preparatory Committee for the World Trade Organization: Draft Report to the WTO (1994), GATT Doc. PC/R/W/1/Rev.2, 16 December.

Raynolds, Laura T., Murray Douglas L. and Wilkinson, John (2007), *Fair Trade: the Challenges of Transforming Globalization,* USA: Routledge.

Reitan, Ruth (2007), "A Global Civil Society in a World Polity, or Angels and Nomads against Empire?" *Global Governance,* 13: 445-60.

Report on the GATT Symposium on Trade, Environment and Sustainable Development (1994), GATT Doc. TE 008, Centre William Rappard, Geneva, 28 July.

Roster of Non-Governmental Panelists (1990), GATT Doc. L/6763, 14 November.

Said, Yahia and Desai, Meghnad (2003), "Trade and Global Civil Society: The Anti-Capitalist Movement Revisited" in Kaldor, Mary, Anheier, Helmut and Glasius, Marlies (eds.) *Global Civil Society 2003.*

Sampson, Gary P. (2001), *The Role of the World Trade Organization in Global Governance,* Tokyo: The United Nations University Press.

Sen, S. R. (1994), "From GATT to WTO", *Economic and Political Weekly,* 29(43), October, 2802-04.

Shaffer, Ellen R. (et.al.) (2005), "Global Trade and Public Health", *American Journal of Public Health,* 95(1), January, 23-34.

Smith, Sally and Barrientos, Stephanie (2005), "Fair Trade and Ethical Trade: Are There Moves towards Convergence?" *Sustainable Development,* 13: 190-98.

Sornarajah, M. (2004), *The International Law on Foreign Investment,* Second Edition, UK: Cambridge University Press.

Spero, Joan Edelman and Hart, Jeffrey A. (2009), *The Politics of International Economic Relations,* USA: Wadsworth.

Understanding Regarding Notification, Consultation, Dispute Settlement and Surveillance, Adopted on 28 November 1979, GATT Doc. L/4907, [Online: web] Accessed 18 November 2009 URL: http://www.wto.org/english/docs_e/legal_e/tokyo_notif_e.pdf.

UN Doc. E/CONF.2/158 (1947) *UN Conference on Trade and Employment: Comments of the International Co-operative Alliance on the Draft Charter of the ITO,* December 1947.

UN Doc. E/PC/T/PV/2 (1946) *Preparatory Committee of the International Conference on Trade and Employment: Verbatim Report of Second Plenary Meeting,* 17 October 1946.

United Nations Non-Governmental Liaison Service (UNNGLS) (2003), "NGOs Assess the Millennium Development Goals", *NGLS Round Up 105,* July.

United Nations Conference on Trade and Development (UNCTAD) (2008), *Globalization for Development: the International Trade Perspective,* Geneva: UN Publication.

UNCTAD/GDS/MDPB/Misc. 14 (2001), *Globalization and the Labour Market,* Paper prepared by the UNCTAD Secretariat for the meeting of the ILO Working Party on the Social Dimension of Globalization, 12 November 2001.

United Nations Conference on Trade and Employment (1948): Final Act and Related Documents, Interim Commission, ICITO, UN Doc. E/Conf. 2/78, April.

Vivekanandan, B. and Giri, DK (2001), *Contemporary Europe and South Asia,* New Delhi: Concept Publishing Company.

Wilkinson, Michael D. (1996), "Lobbying for Fair Trade: Northern NGDOs, the European Community and the GATT Uruguay Round", *Third World Quarterly,* 17(2), 251-67.

Wilson, Robert R. (1947), "Toward a World Conference on Trade and Employment", *The American Journal of International Law,* January, 41(1): 127-31.

World Trade Organization (WTO) (2001), *Dictionary of Trade Policy Terms: Fourth Edition,* UK: Cambridge University Press.

World Trade Organization (WTO), "Six Decades of Multilateral Trade Cooperation: What Have We Learnt? *World Trade Report 2007.*

World Fair Trade Organization Annual Report 2009, Netherland: WFTO Publications.

WTO Annual Report 2007, Geneva: WTO Publications.

The Opening of Pandora's Box: The U.S.-India Civilian Nuclear Technology Deal

Rajit H. Das

Abstract

My paper, The Opening of Pandora's Box: The U.S.-Civilian Nuclear Technology Deal sets the precedence for an emerging conflict that going to be researched. This conflict is considered to be the rebirth of a new, more serious Cold War that has already begun to escalate between India and Pakistan and can potentially expand to one with India and China. With the passage of the nuclear accord, China and Pakistan have become concerned about the strengthening of the bilateral relationship being enhanced economically, strategically, and defensively deals through deals between the United States and India. This paper will explore the various aspects to the accord. Furthermore, it will go to show how the United States is being contradictory to its own nuclear policy (Non Proliferation Treaty, Comprehensive Test Ban Treaty). This paper will also illustrate Pakistan's insecurity, the Chinese dimension, the role of the United States, and India's position with regards to nuclear weapons and technology. Finally, the paper will prove how Indian government has a mind of its own, irrespective of how concerns expressed by China, Pakistan, and the United States.

THE OPENING OF PANDORA'S BOX: The U.S-India Civilian Nuclear Technology Deal

The United States ushered in a new era with the passage of the Henry J. Hyde Civilian Nuclear Technology deal with India. This deal strengthened the bilateral relationship between the two democracies. This agreement, in combination with defense deals through their bilateral relationship, brought forth Pakistan's insecurity. The worry in the world is that Pakistan's arsenal of nuclear weapons is not secured, and terrorists residing in the country can access to them to use against their enemies, primarily India. The world is also well aware of the problems found in Pakistan. India and Pakistan having nuclear weapons raises serious issues of what would happen in case of war. To the rest of the world, however, the prospect of an exchange of nuclear missiles between the two neighbors, whose deadliest weapons could reach each other capitals and major cities in less than ten minutes, was too terrifying to contemplate (Wolpert, 2011).

This paper will explore how the Civilian Nuclear Technology Agreement was born, how it was changed, how the strategic relationships between the two countries were formulated, and the concerns that arise with the passage of such an historic deal. In addition, the paper will go to show the spillover effects the nuclear accord gave birth to. Finally, this paper will go to prove that the United States is playing the role of the instigator to destabilize the already fragile Asian regional stability by unnecessarily causing alarm for both China and Pakistan through the passage of the nuclear accord.

Civilian Nuclear Technology Agreement: The Origins

The Bush administration pushed the agreement on the basis of non-proliferation for India. Because most of India's energy-generating reactors were not under international monitoring and, thus, the reactors could be used for military purposes, the Bush administration wanted India to place reactors under "safeguards" by which they would be subject to international monitoring

and inspection (Mistry, 2006). In addition to the non-proliferation benefits, the Bush

administration campaigned actively in Congress for other such "benefits", including   promoting

a stable balance of power, strengthening U.S.-India ties, placing India's civilian nuclear facilities

under safeguards, and adopting stronger export controls that would bring it into compliance

(Mistry, 2006). Furthermore, a new push in enhanced strategic relations between United States

and India came with the agreement. A lot of commentary came from scholars on the emerging

relationship was being made. According to Even A. Feigenbaum (2010), the future scope of U.S.

- Indian relationship will depend on choices made both in Washington and New Delhi; the

United States looks to India to sustain its economic and social change while still embracing a

partnership with Washington, and India looks to the United States to respect Indian security

concerns.

During the intense negotiations, the United States made a pressing case for India. In the

2005 agreement, the United States accommodated to India in two important ways: first, without

giving India formal status as a nuclear weapons state, Washington, nonetheless, acknowledged

that, " [a]s responsible state with a advanced nuclear technology, India should acquire the same

benefits and advantages as other states" (Mistry, 2006). Second, and more substantively, the

Bush administration agreed to assist India in obtaining civilian nuclear technology by, in part,

seeking an "agreement from Congress to adjust U.S. laws and policies" to help facilitate

technology transfers and cooperation (Mistry, 2006). The push from the Bush administration was

fruitful for the agreement. The Bush administration pursued negotiations on many fronts—with

Congress, the Nuclear Suppliers Group [NSG], and India. India also began to secure approval for

nuclear transfers into the country. In December 2006, the U.S Congress by an overwhelming vote, gave conditional approval to the nuclear cooperation deal and made broad U.S. civilian nuclear energy exports legal for the first time (Fitzpatrick, 2008). However, not all of the contentious issues of the agreement were resolved, and deliberations s continued, between United States and India.

Civilian Nuclear Technology Agreement: Motivations

The United States and India shared similar goals with regards to this agreement and, hence, pushed forward with it. The Bush administration has argued, with some justification, that the nuclear accord would impose a greater degree of transparency on India's nuclear program than had previously existed and that the upgrading of India's civilian nuclear power would help reduce dependence on fossil fuels. Therefore, there was arguably more ambitious strategic and economic considerations were behind the U.S.-India nuclear accord (Sharma, 2009). In addition, it did not threaten American interests (Ganguly and Mukherji, 2011). Overall, the United States looked to it as a business opportunity. Economically, India represents a lucrative and fast-growing market for American businesses, including producers of dual use technology (Tellis, 2006). Bush agreed to negotiate a deal that would allow American firms to export technology worth billions to India, along with nuclear expertise (Sanger, 2009).

India does have its energy needs. The goals that India and the United States created affected their respective strategic relations with China. The Bush administration remained convinced that the agreement with India would eventually be passed because it was a cornerstone of India's new security strategy and important to the United States in its efforts to balance a rising China (Sharma, 2009). As Singh notes, to the Indian strategy policy makers, ending the "nuclear apartheid" would not only open up new and important avenues of economic, strategic, and diplomatic cooperation, but the American offer of strategic partnership would also encourage China to continue improving relations with India (Sharma, 2009). For India, the goal of this agreement was in the name of development because the energy crisis grew at an alarming rate. To tackle this, the weak energy sector needed to be stronger to meet the needs of the Indian citizens, as seen in India's position. The strategic relationship that India had with America was watched closely by China.

Civilian Nuclear Technology Agreement: Criticisms

Even if India's goal was worthwhile, in the beginning, the nuclear agreement faced severe backlash from the opposition parties and domestic critics skeptical of the agreement because it was in the United States by the non-proliferation lobbyists. India's opposition parties initially objected to the fact because by opening India's nuclear sector to inspections, the U.S.-India agreement would restrict India's sovereignty and its sovereign right to independent nuclear decision-making. Domestic critics [i.e. from Parliament] noted this U.S.-instigated moratorium was equivalent to India accepting the Comprehensive Test Ban Treaty and it would potentially prevent India from countering any nuclear tests by either Pakistan or China (Mistry, 2006). Meanwhile, as the agreement evolved, opposition was seen in the Obama administration. In the United States, the main opposition groups were the non-proliferation lobbyists, which were successful in dealing with the Obama administration to implement measures within the existing agreement to prevent India from using the agreement as a loophole to stock pile on nuclear weapons. Because nuclear reprocessing involves separating and processing spent fuel, including that which is potentially weapons grade, the Obama administration insisted on putting place an inspection regime designed to prevent India from ever diverting U.S.- supplied nuclear fuel to its military program (Sharma, 2011). Hence, the criticisms for the nuclear accord came from the Bush administration and carried over to the Obama administration.

Criticisms were stronger in the Bush administration than during the Obama administration. The fact that Pakistan's demand for equal treatment was rejected by the Bush administration because of the proliferation activities of Pakistani nuclear scientist A.Q Khan is hardly a reason to celebrate; Pakistan could seek a similar agreement with China (Sharma, 2009). Furthermore, they contend that the accord sets a bad precedent because it has the potential to encourage others nations to demand similar deals (Sharma, 2009). However, India's assurance was known to the United States, and the United States knew that India was a responsible nuclear power. Even then, the restrictions to the original Hyde Act were no longer a barrier for India. When the NSG approved a new policy under which India could receive nuclear and uranium from all its members, the restrictions in the Hyde Act became politically irrelevant because France and Russia could now supply India with nuclear technology and materials in the event of another nuclear test, even if the United States cut off nuclear cooperation (Sagan, 2009). It could be said that the true benefactor of the nuclear accord was India because it put India into the forefront to engage itself into the market for nuclear energy.

The only option now was the passage of the act, taking everything into consideration. It still can be seen as a contradictory for the United States to allow India to develop civilian nuclear technology with the "potential" to produce nuclear weapons but not by the "axis of evil". The "axis of evil" refers to countries that the Bush administration deemed a threat to the United States. These countries possessed nuclear weapons or were trying to acquire nuclear weapons that could be used against the United States. Countries on the list, for example, are North Korea and Iran. The strongest opposition was seen from China, which also reflects this double standard shown by the United States. Although Beijing's official reaction has been measured, unofficially, its disapproval of Washington's double standard in its non-proliferation policy (e.g. punishing

Iran and North Korea for their nuclear programs while facilitating a deal for a non-NPT [Non Proliferation Treaty] signatory was duly noted (Sharma, 2009).

Civilian Nuclear Technology Agreement: Passage with Additional Bill

Before to the final passage of the bill in 2006, there was a compromise that was made. India's nuclear separation plan struck a balance between Washington's position, which was influenced by U.S. domestic lobbies, and that India position, influenced by its nuclear scientists, of keeping key facilities away from international inspections (Mistry, 2006). Later on, in 2008, the final contentious issue was resolved that was briefly mentioned earlier in the paper. It came from the United States. Specifically, the U.S., demanded that India establish an supplier liability in case of a nuclear accident before agreeing to do business in India (Sharma, 2011). From India, the legislative passage of a "Civilian Nuclear Liability Regime" limited the liability of American companies operating in India (Sharma, 2011). In fact, Bush and his chief negotiator, Nicholas Burns, were never able to extract a promise from the Indians that in return for American assistance, they would stop producing weapons – grade nuclear fuel and stop expanding their arsenal (Sanger, 2009). It is imperative to have the new bill in place to finally implement the Civilian Nuclear Liability Bill in India. Indians debated in Parliament, and the law was passed in August 25, 2008, for the Civilian Nuclear Liability Bill (Sharma, 2011). Finally, this brought the Henry J. Hyde Civilian Nuclear Technology deal into force.

CHINESE DIMENSION

Although the U.S.-India nuclear technology deal does not directly involve China, it has a tremendous influence on the the strategic relations the two countries have with China. The passage of the agreement has resulted in complicated relations that China has with India,

Pakistan, and the United States. The Chinese were apprehensive towards it. The country has a careful watch and is being calculative in the way it handles relations with "all parties" involved directly and indirectly. This takes place through its bilateral relations and diplomatic involvement in the NSG and International Atomic Energy Agency [IAEA]. As a member of both the IAEA and NSG, Beijing approval is essential to take the Indo-U.S. nuclear deal forward; after receiving approval from the IAEA, India would have to obtain a waver by consensus from the NSG to allow nuclear commerce with the international community (Sharma, 2009). Moreover, China recognized the potential far reaching impact of the U.S.-India nuclear agreement on the strategic balance of power in Asia (Sharma, 2009).

The civilian nuclear technology deal exacerbates tensions between India and Pakistan. This deal has direct implications in the nuclear policies of India and Pakistan. The conflict in Kashmir is what all of this is related to. The potential for war is imminent, and China recognizes the threat it plays to Asian regional stability. Hence, China deals with Pakistan cautiously as illustrated below. Against this background and cognizant of the fact that a regional Indo-Pakistani war can unwittingly drag China into conflict, Beijing's security relationship with Pakistan has become more nuanced, if not cautious (Sharma, 2009). China is also aware of Pakistan's on the ground realities, its affect on escalating the conflict with India, and the ramifications that can come from a nuclear war between the two countries. Beijing primary (and valid) concern is that given Pakistan's weak command and control structure of its nuclear facilities and its "first use" doctrine, an inadvertent use of nuclear weapons could result in a deadly escalation engulfing the region and beyond (Sharma, 2009).

The Pakistani Insecurity Nexus between the India and the United States

The Pakistani position on the U.S.-India Civilian Nuclear Technology Deal with India is simple-- it only increases Pakistan's insecurity with India. The stronger U.S. – India strategic relationship is, especially within the defense sector, the more it is a threat to Pakistan's national security. More importantly, both in the short term and long term, is the India-U.S. agreement to cooperate on missile defense, with the acquisition of missile defense capability by India, directly destabilizes the nuclear deterrence in South Asia, as well as undermining Pakistan's doctrine of minimum deterrence and nuclear restraint (Mazari). In the case for the use of nuclear weapons, to sustain a credible defense, Pakistan will have to begin multiplying its missiles and warheads very soon... (Mazari). [Finally,] the "minimum deterence" will be moved to a much higher level unless Pakistan also acquires missile defense capabilities (Mazari). The pressure to develop Pakistan weapons system is escalated through defense deals between the United States and India.

Pakistan's position on the nuclear front is completely against India. Nuclear weapons were seen as a way of countering India's larger army, matching India's suspected nuclear program (the original intention of Pakistan with the creation of its nuclear program) and providing an umbrella under which Pakistan might launch low-level probes in the disputed Kashmir region (Cohen, 2004). In recent years, it is no wonder no other country has been as concerned, for obvious reasons, about India's growing conventional military strength and nuclear capability as Pakistan (Rais, 2005). Aside from the growing bilateral relationship now between India and the United States, what will be assessed is Pakistan's national security policy and how it is tied down to its nuclear policy. For over a half a century, Pakistan's security dilemma has centered on how to balance, counter, and if necessary, fight the Indian threat (Rais, 2005). India has defeated Pakistan in four wars fought in 1947, 1965, 1971, and 1998. As a result, this also heightens Pakistan's insecurity levels. However, Pakistan uses it to their advantage. It has very effectively used the geopolitics of the region and history of the conflict with India to present itself as a threatened, insecure, and vulnerable, requiring strong military power, including nuclear capabilities, to defend its nation and statehood (Rais, 2005). In addition, the nuclear danger draws international attention, potentially securing for weaker Pakistan third-party mediation of its territorial dispute with India and a diplomatic settlement superior to any that Pakistan alone could achieve (Sagan, 2009). The nuclear bomb for Pakistan has been embedded into its national identity because the nuclear bomb is seen as the absolute weapon with which to defend the territoriality of the sub-continental Muslim nationalism that Pakistan as a nation state embodies. (Rais, 2005). The nuclear bomb represents the only viable weapon that can be used against India, though it never has in the past wars. Pakistan got nuclear weapons in the 1970s. Military leaders concluded that nuclear weapons were the cheapest, most effective, and reliable route to national security (Rais, 2005). Later on, the nuclear doctrine for the nation was established. According to Pakistan, a rough nuclear parity is the best guarantee of peace and stability in the region (Rais, 2005).

Pakistan's nuclear doctrine has been interpreted differently by scholars. The body of research for which this section is based upon offers the counter-argument that differs from American views. Accordingly, the central assumption around which Pakistan has built up its nuclear capability is that a credible nuclear deterrent would compensate for the inferiority of its conventional forces, and, therefore, Pakistan also considers that nuclear deterrence means to offset Indian conventional superiority (Rais, 2005). One of the fundamental elements of a credible nuclear deterrence is the belief that both sides in a nuclear equation have destructive nuclear forces that can convincingly be delivered, even after absorbing a first strike, and that they can inflict an unacceptable level of damage on the adversary (Rais, 2005). Pakistan, therefore, acknowledges what India is capable of doing and is well aware of its options in case of a nuclear confrontation with India. Another factor that requires investigation is the concept of minimum deterrence, and how it can be found in Pakistan's nuclear doctrine. The minimum deterrence posture is associated with the notion of sufficiency of nuclear forces, meaning these forces are sufficient to survive a first strike and stage a counter-strike, and Pakistan is currently pursuing minimum deterrence (Rais, 2005).

There is a lot of controversy surrounding Pakistan's nuclear weapons program. Strategic analysts, such as Vernie Liebel of Booze Allen Hamilton, think otherwise. Pakistan has developed an India-centric deterrent based on the doctrine of "first use" to ensure ambiguity (Liebel, 2009). Pakistan's nuclear deterrent is heavily dependent upon China for technology and maintenance (Liebel, 2009). As India goes to America for defense deals and weapons technology, Pakistan goes to China. This is the brunt of all the problems. Looking further into the assessment, Liebel makes the following observations: Pakistan has no official nuclear deterrence or employment (Liebel, 2009). Furthermore, Pakistan intent is to initiate the use of nuclear weapons in response to nuclear or "conventional" aggression and has reserved the right to preemptively use nuclear weapons in response to what it deems as threatening moves by India (Liebel, 2009). America's position towards Pakistan is quite apprehensive, and it raises alarms to what India has been suggesting all along in regards to Pakistan's nuclear ambitions. When revisiting everything, what makes Pakistan stance especially alarming is best described by Liebel, in that what Pakistan deems as threatening move has been left deliberately ambiguous (Liebel, 2009). By not having a clear set of guidelines allows Pakistan to potentially use nuclear weapons indiscriminately. Pakistan's views of what is acceptable to warrant the use of nuclear weapons is described as "red-lines," as shown by Liebel, which to India should be seen as a significant threat. The most important "red-lines" are illustrated below and they describe

Pakistan nuclear deterrent ability by set forth by Lieutenant General Khalid Kidwai, Director of the Strategic Plan of Pakistan nuclear command structure, in addition to other "red-lines", as suggested by Pakistan military officers.

1) India attacks Pakistan and conquers a large part of territory.

2) India pushes Pakistan into political destabilization or creates large-scale internal subversion Indian crossing the Line of Control (LOC) to an extent that threatens Pakistan's control of Azad Kashmir.

3) An attack of any of Pakistan's power generation facilities or nuclear installations.

(Liebel, 2009)

These red lines show how Pakistan's nuclear policy is geared only to the Indian threat. Pakistan remains reactive to India, and thus, its development of missile force is India-centric, all of its nuclear delivery means are designed to reach targets in India, the only country that Pakistan believes threatens it (Liebel, 2009). Pakistan's strategic interest are weapons technology similar to what India has received. Pakistan has developed its nuclear weapons illegitimately through the workings of A.Q Khan. But, the diabolical way was envisioned by him was because of India's acquisition of advanced weaponry, including nuclear. Pakistan would be at major disadvantage in a conventional war with India, which had a two-to-one advantage in troops. (Woodward, 2010). As a result, Pakistan did not want to be pressed to halt their production of fissile material for more nuclear weapons (Woodward, 2010).

The Role of the United States

Diplomatically, it encourages India and Pakistan to resolve issues which threaten the use of nuclear weapons, yet its back-door policy with these countries suggests otherwise. Under the umbrella of nuclear policy, it is also important to remember that India and Pakistan still have not resolved the conflict in Kashmir, and another war in that region could prompt the use of nuclear weapons (or threat) as it did in 1998, when the United States intervened through diplomatic sanctions with both countries and ended it. However, even if the United States did not intervene, both countries would have still practiced restraint.

Chellaney (1998-1999) argues that India nuclear tests caused both the United States and China began to take seriously as a rising power (Sharma, 2009). What we expect nuclear deterrents is the prevention of outbreak of total war because of the inherent risks of escalation to nuclear exchanges, which in the case of India and Pakistan could be suicidal (Rais, 2005). In this case, the United States directly has a direct position and role in it. Both countries are watching how the United States plays its cards. The difficulty of being in this predicament has been expressed by Admiral Richard Wallard, commander of the United States Asian Pacific Command, while testifying before the Senate Arms committee. "Securing Pakistani regional cooperation while placating India is a difficult task. Pakistani officials seek a long term bilateral relationship with the U.S. based on regional vision conducive to Pakistani strategic interests" (Haniffa, 2011).

The United States is aware of this complicated and complex nexus but is taking advantage of it. There is an assumption that is carried by the Americans that also has been factored into the equation. Many Americans (leaders) look to a new partnership with India to be a bulwark against China and an ally in the effort to curb Iranian nuclear ambitions (Fitzpatrick, 2008). As noted earlier, Pakistan is weary of U.S. involvement in military weapons sales with India. Similarly, India is weary of fighting the Taliban and militants in regards to the global war on terrorism. Both countries are taking advantage of the situation, and hence, there is no resolution in sight. Under the disguise of defense deals, the United States is single-handedly involved with the India-Pakistan imbroglio, all for its business interests. The U.S. Civilian Nuclear Technology Agreement and the defense contracts its signs with India are hallmark examples of this. Dealing with Pakistan has been difficult for the United States. For all the public talk about democracy and development and the need to foster moderation in Pakistani society, in the end, it's the security of the arsenal that captivates Washington's attention. (Sanger, 2009). Both administrations faced hard times predicting Pakistan's future. The fact is the Bush administration didn't know what would happen to the nuclear weapons if Pakistan dissolved into chaos, and neither will Obama (Sanger, 2009). The fact still remains that Pakistan is the only nuclear state with powerful insurgency in the midst, one that clearly has aims to take over the country and desperately wants to acquire the nuclear bomb (Sanger, 2009). Also, every kilogram of nuclear fuel that the United States sold to the Indians to use in their power plants freed up some fuel to make more weapons (Sanger, 2009).

Political Implications and the Global War on Terror

What is so ironic to see is that even though there was bickering by both parties during the negotiations about the passage of the bill, key politicians in both parties, including the presidential candidates of the 2008 elections, all supported the bill. For their part, both U.S. presidential candidates, Senator John McCain and Senator Barack Obama, praised the NSG for allowing its members to engage in nuclear cooperation with India, and both candidates urged the U.S. Congress to quickly pass the U.S-India Agreement for Civil Nuclear Cooperation (Sharma, 2009). In fact, their concerted efforts paid off: on October 2, 2008, the India – U.S. nuclear deal secured the approval of the U.S. Senate, which voted overwhelmingly in favor of the accord

(Sharma, 2009). An interesting revelation that came out of this would be that all three senators directly involved in the presidential race – (Barack Obama, Joe Biden, and John McCain) voted for the bill (Sharma, 2009).

The global war on terrorism was started in the Bush administration and got carried over into the Obama administration. President Obama, in the beginning of this tenure as president, began to deliberate on how to deal with Pakistan under the auspices of this war. Irrespective, of how much cooperation Pakistan had with the United States in their campaign against terrorism through counter-insurgency operations, the Pakistani government continued to support terrorist groups, such as the LeT (Lashkar – e – Taiba), who was engaging a different type of campaign against India trying to make it a Sharia state. The last major terrorist attack occurred November 26, 2008 in Mumbai. The LeT was responsible for the attack, the group received training from Al Qaeda to carry out the terrorist attack. The United States under the Obama administration, had to deal with Pakistan, and at the same time not irritate India. Bob Woodward, in his book *Obama's Wars*, described it. Bruce Reidel, a South Asian security expert, discussed Pakistan and the links the country had to terrorist organizations with President Obama. If there was another attack on U.S. soil, Obama had a plan (Woodward, 2010). In addition, Reidel incorporated another facet to President Obama in their discussions of how to deal with Pakistan in the global war on terror by presenting a different scenario to the president. "Pakistan attacks India again, either directly or indirectly, Mumbai redux. What are we going to do to the Indians this time? We admire your Gandhi –like self restraint. I think we probably researched the threshold in India," Reidel said. The next attack will get a military response. And that means you're talking about a potential for nuclear war (Woodward, 2010). It can be said once again, that the United

States is cognizant of the realities but, instead, accepts the risks when carrying out the relationship it has with Pakistan.

The global war on terrorism was fought on two fronts. The first one being in Afghanistan, and was later shifted to the second front, Iraq. The Indians got the confidence from what the United States did in the name of national security. The world came to learn of the illegitimate reasons why the United States invaded Iraq. India took advantage of the situation and got the confidence to create its own doctrine of preventive strike on Pakistan, if warranted (Sagan, 2009). Following the U.S. invasion of Iraq, Indian foreign minister ,Yashwant Sinha, claimed that his country reserved the right to use force against Pakistan, stating " There were three reasons which drove the Anglo-US forces to attack Iraq: possession of weapons of mass destruction, export of terrorism, and an absence of democracy all of which exist in Pakistan" (Sagan, 2009). This preemptive strike which India could potentially make towards Pakistan could even be done with a launch of nuclear weapons into Pakistan to stop it once and for all. The Obama administration even predicted it, as illustrated in the previous paragraph. Yet, it is a noteworthy change in Indian strategic debates that senior Indian politicians could hint – after years of statements about defense doctrines, no first use, and principles of nonaggression – that an Indian preemptive strike against Pakistan could be justified (Sagan, 2009). India has been tested by Pakistan time and again. Even after this statement was announced by India and the security analysis done by the Obama administration in the previous paragraph, India still has not gone forth with one. This reiteration makes one ask, what will compel India to do it, if not for what has already been done to India by Pakistan? When is it enough is for India? In a different way, it is imperative for the United States to rethink its policies towards India, because the evidence provided gives proof that a whole new conflict, an Asian or South Asian Cold War, is in the horizon, affecting all major power players of the region. This is the direct threat to Asian regional stability.

Spillover Effects

India apparently believes its current nuclear dyad is inadequate and is seeking to emplace a nuclear triad and associated doctrine, similar to that of the U.S. and Russian nuclear triad (Liebel, 2009). Moreover, this developing "doctrine" is combined with the geostrategic neighborhood that India lives in and has guided development of India's nuclear force structure (Liebel, 2009). Finally, India is seeking to develop a nuclear triad for an increased survivability of its nuclear force (Liebel, 2009). India's position is shaped by its position it has thus far militarily against Pakistan and China. The need for India to advance its position militarily, comes from how it views the condition of its neighbors and their strategic moves.

According to Kapur (1998), nuclear tests had a lot of meaning for the Indians. The Vajpayee government proclaimed that India was a now a full-fledged nuclear weapons state and maintained that the tests were necessary to protect India's national security, especially against the Chinese threat (Sagan, 2009). However, it was not explicitly stated by India; it also was a wake-up call to Pakistan of India's capabilities once again. By showing it now had a viable nuclear deterrent, India finally laid to rest the reputation of weakness that has long bedeviled it, that is, its structural weaknesses and an inability to project power (Sharma, 2009). Finally, with the tests, India served notice that it now possessed the material capabilities to match its bold aspirations (Basrur, 2006). Yet, India test had given the army, and A.Q. Khan the political cover they needed to demonstrate their technical accomplishment (Sagan, 2009). In addition, Pakistani authorities could claim that they were merely responding to provocations from the Indians, who had gone first (Sagan, 2009). The above descriptions found in this paragraph were stated to reflect the viewpoints on the 1998 nuclear tests conducted on the onslaught of war in Kargil fought by both countries in Kashmir. However, looking back into history, the above analysis possesses a warning to what could be if nothing is done to deter India and Pakistan from advancing into another arms race. As stated by Robert Sanger in his book, *The Inheritance*, Pakistan, of course, vowed that if the Indians built more weapons, so would they (Sanger, 2009). Bush, in short accelerated the arms race in South Asia (Sanger, 2009).

It is interesting to see how India watches how the United States reacts, in regards to testing its own nuclear weapons. The United States has not tested one since the trying times of World War II, yet India aspires to do so following the behavior of the "model country". It is no surprise, with respects to testing, that National Security Advisory Board [NSAB] recommended, according to press reports, that India should resume testing nuclear devices if the U.S. resumes its own nuclear tests." (Roche, 2003). It is highly revealing that for the NSAB, the trigger for resumption of nuclear testing was not that China or Pakistan had started to test nuclear weapons, but, rather the U.S. resumption of testing (Sagan, 2009). Hence, to India, if the U.S. could do it, so could India.

The Cold War of the Past and the Cold War of the Present

At the conclusion of World War II, the Cold War of the past came. This Cold War was fought between the United States and Soviet Union. Both countries possessed nuclear weapons. The world knew of the cataclysmic effects of a nuclear weapon. After all, the United States dropped it in Hiroshima and Nagasaki. The United States did everything in its power to stop the spread of communism. This war was war between democracy and communism. In the midst of this, there was a nuclear arms race that was fueled by both countries stockpiling on weapons (ICBMs and nukes) aimed at each other. As described by Stanley Wolpert in his book, *India and Pakistan*, four decades of a 'mutually assured destruction' (MAD) Cold War between the United States and the Soviet Union had served to dispel most fears of a nuclear war, which had to be regarded as highly, unlikely (Wolpert, 2011).   Ironically, the Cuban Missile Crisis served as a lasting reminder of this. In addition, these superpowers, however, were more remote from each other than India and Pakistan, and they had developed more nuclear safeguards and effective early warning systems than have as yet been introduced or mutually accepted in South Asia (Wolpert, 2011).

In South Asia, the Cold War between India and Pakistan was borne after India test fired its first nuclear bomb. The Indians had a head start in May 1974, with Prime Minister, Indira Gandhi, as a witness, and had conducted their first nuclear test (Sanger, 2009). The Indians called it a "peaceful explosion," but because the test was conducted within a hundred miles of the Pakistani border, the message was short of subtle (Sanger, 2009). Consider, then, this nuclear test as a threat and warning to Pakistan of Indian capabilities. To Musharaff, a young officer rising through the army ranks at the time, the Indian test left Pakistan so vulnerable that "our strategy of minimal deterrence was undermined, was compromised" (Sanger, 2009). Hence, it did not take long, he said before "we [Pakistan] decided that we had to go nuclear" (Sanger, 2009). The Cold War was now being played at a more hostile level. Because of the unrelenting case that India and Pakistan continue to have so many misgivings, be it the conflict in Kashmir to terrorism, this Cold War should be considered the next greatest threat to destabilize the Asian regional stability that the United States is responsible for perpetuating with their relationship with India. Therefore, with India having the capability of producing more nuclear weapons, coupled with the fact that although India has declared it seeks only minimal credible deterrence, it has never specified their level of nuclear armament, further intensifying the two way nuclear arms race between India and Pakistan and India and China (Sharma, 2009). If not anything else, this should be considered a wake-up call to the United States to reassess how it deals with their relationship with China and Pakistan, in that working in the same capacity as India and United States can lead to more conflict if not dealt with appropriately.

Conclusion

The United States is complicating the situation by meddling in the waters through defense contracts and other incentives to India in the interest of business and trade. The economic opportunity costs of developing a substantial nuclear weapons program in a country that, despite a recent spurt of economic growth, still faces the challenge of addressing the problem of endemic rural and urban poverty are hardly trivial (Ganguly, 2008). Money that is used to develop this should be allocated to other much urgent needs. The United States should facilitate this change of action through backing down from bilateral agreements that increase insecurity in Pakistan. The short term benefits for India that were envisioned by the Civilian Nuclear Technology Deal resulted in a increased level of insecurity by Pakistan and the remission of nuclear proliferation from both countries. Furthermore, the Indians, by contrast, believe that the lesson of the South Asian nuclear crisis is that India must be prepared to fight a limited, conventional conflict under a nuclear umbrella (Sagan, 2009). The United States has to act without inflaming the sentiments of both countries. The Chinese are catching onto the motives of the United States and, therefore, developing their bilateral relationship with Pakistan. In other words, the United States is appeasing both India and Pakistan at two different levels. As a result, it has been proven that Pakistan has taken advantage of it. Meanwhile, India is using its trump card. If the United States doesn't provide it with its needs, India can go somewhere else. The U.S.-India Civilian Nuclear Technology deal was an attempt by the U.S. to nurture the growing relationship that the two countries have.

However, the nurturing relationship has been diabolical in the eyes of the United States adversaries, Pakistan and China, to a different nature. Could it be that the United States is playing the role of a hypocrite? Non-proliferation has been one of the platforms that the United States foreign policy is based upon, and it ironically encourages nuclear proliferation in Pakistan and India. It is blatantly clear that Pakistan resorts to nuclear weapons as a deterrent to India. The United States is instigating a bigger conflict that can further destabilize Asian regional stability as it attempts to be the counterweight to China by developing the stronger relationship with India. Therefore, Pakistan is the sacrificial knight that is used by the United States and China, and India is the coveted king that China and United States both want possession of. The only problem is that it is not easily done as it seems because this king has a mind of his own that the world can certainly see.

BIBLIOGRAPHY

Basrur, R. M. (2006). *Minimum deterence and indian nuclear security*. Stanford, CA: Stanford University Press.

Cohen, S. (2004). *The idea of pakistan*. Washington, DC: Brookings Institution Press.

Feigenbaum, E. (2010). India's rise, america's interest. *Foreign Affairs*, *89*(2), 76-91.

Fitzpatrick, M. (2008). Us - india nuclear cooperation accord: implications for non proliferation regime. *Asia-Pacific Review*, *15*(1), 76-85.

Ganguly, S. (2008). War, nuclear weapons, and crisis stability in south asia. *Security Studies*, *17*, 164-184.

Ganguly, S., & Mukherji, R. (2011). *India since 1980*. Cambridge, UK: Cambridge University Press.

Haniffa, A. (2011, April 13). Indo-pak impasse unlikely to end soon: u.s. *India Abroad*, Retrieved from http://www.rediff.com/news/report/indo-pak-impasse-unlikely-to-end-soon-says- us/20110413.htm

Liebel, V. (2009). India and pakistan: competing nuclear strategies and doctrines. *Comparative Strategy*, *28*, 154-163.

Mazari, S. South asian security: international context. *Policy Perspectives*, *3*(1),

Mistry, D. (2006). Diplomacy, domestic policies, and the u.s.-india nuclear agreement. *Asian Survey*, *XLVI*(5), 675-696.

Rais, R. (2005). Conceptualizing nuclear detterence: pakistan's posture. *India Review*, *4*(2), 144-172

Roche, E. (2003, January 13). India evaluating, fine-tuning nuclear doctrine, experts say. *Hong kong agency france press*. Retrieved from http://toolkit.dia.log.com/intranet/cgi/present? STYLE=739318018&PRESENT=DB=985,AN=165050958,FM=9,SEARCH=MD.Gener icSearch.

Sagan, S. D. (2009). *Inside nuclear south asia*. Stanford, CA: Stanford University Press.

Sanger, D. E. (2009). *The inheritance: The world obama confronts and the challenges to american power*. New York: Harmony Books.

Sharma, S. (2009). *China and india in the age of globalization*. Cambridge, UK: Cambridge University Press.

Sharma, S. (2011). India in 2010. *Asian Survey, 51*(1), 111-124.

Tellis, A. J. (2006). *India and a new global power: an agenda for the united states*. Washington, DC: Carnegie Endowment for International Peace.

Wolpert, S. (2011). *India and pakistan: Continued conflict or cooperation*. Berkeley, CA: University of California Press.

Woodward, B. (2010). *Obama's wars* . New York, NY: Simon & Schuster.

An Analysis of Prospect Theory

Bina Patel, PhD

Abstract

The purpose of this paper is to offer an analysis Jack Midlarsky's article Loss Aversion, Framing Effects, and International Conflict. This paper will present the concepts and findings of prospect theory. Also, this paper will illustrate the phases of prospect theory in relation to international war and terrorism.

Wars can be perceived as a consequence of state greed. Terrorism has become a consequence of wars. Also, the new normalcy has become that terrorist organizations are born at the time of war to defend their enemy within their land. The purpose of this paper is to offer an analysis Jack Midlarsky's article *Loss Aversion, Framing Effects, and International Conflict.* This paper will present the concepts and findings of prospect theory. Also, this paper will illustrate the phases of prospect theory in relation to international war and terrorism.

Prospect theory is a theory developed to be used to help make decisions. Decisions can be made at the micro or macro levels. At the micro level, decisions are made for individual purposes. At the macro level, decisions are made at the international level. Throughout this essay, several examples in relation to international war and terrorism will be used to further justify the concepts of prospect theory.

Five primary concepts related to prospect theory further present a full explanation of this ideology. Campbell (2012) provides an insight into the history of the theory. The first concept of prospect theory is that it was developed by Kahneman and Tversky in 1979 to measure the risk associated with decision making. Originally this theory was derived from the utility theory. The utility theory also measures decision making under risk (Campbell, 2012). However, prospect theory is an alternative theory to decision making. The primary purpose of the prospect theory is to provide a set of educated guesses on the behavior of foreign states. The interaction amongst the states within the international system is also measured with prospect theory (Levy, 2000). The theory is also used to provide a descriptive model of economic interactions amongst states.

The second concept of prospect theory is that it is an inductive process. The gains and losses that are predicted or assessed are inductive to decision making. The strategic decisions made are based on the persuasion of the objectives that have been assessed. For instance, within the international system, if a country needs to strategically borrow money to save its economy, it will assess the gains and losses before requesting the money. Any borrowing can cause a trickle affect on another country. For instance, Spain recently has requested to borrow several million Euros from the European Union. The state is facing a second recession after its large debt. The current debt that exists is well over twenty million Euros (Chapple, 2012).

However, Spain has requested to borrow additional funds to the European Union to save its economy for an additional three months. If the European Union allows Spain to borrow the money, it too could result in a large deficit. This deficit in turn would cause a negative economic reaction against its other member states, and potentially the United States (Chapple, 2012). Therefore, it would be vital for both Spain and the European Union to assess the gains and losses before finalizing a decision. In this case, the prospect theory would assist to identify the gains and losses. Once the latter has been identified, then the European Union will be able to make its decision on whether or not to allow Spain to borrow additional funds. This example identifies that prospect theory is a persuasive ideology used as a tool for decision making (Campbell, 2012).

The third concept of prospect theory includes the notion of risk. The judgments that are made under the risk conditions are based on the assessments of the international system. It is important to note that the judgments made are also referred to as gains or losses associated with making a decision. Prospect theory further attempts to help make these assessments. In prospect theory, the judgments or decisions are made during uncertain conditions, consequences or outcomes (Campbell, 2012). Generally, decisions are made with the use of prospect theory when they involve complex conflict.

For example, prior to the Iraq invasion, the United States in 2003 created a strategic plan based upon the assessed judgments. Their judgments were measured in relation to their plan, which was then executed into action. The latter included a war with Iraq (White, 2012). The plan that was created prior to attacking Iraq was justified based on the risks associated with entering the country. Since the war took place after the September 11th attacks against the United States, the risk associated with attacking Iraq included increased domestic terrorism. It is important to note that the September 11th attacks against the United States was a plot developed by Al Qaeda. Al Qaeda is a terrorist group that had organized the hijackings of United States' airplanes. The planes were used to crash into the World Trade Centers in New York City, where thousands of individuals were killed (Campbell, 2012). Other planes were also hijacked in the United States the same day. The primary point is to understand that the negative implications associated with the term terrorism has further convoluted any attempts to arrive at an objective definition (Campbell, 2012). Therefore, any association with terrorism initiates a risk..

In addition, domestic terrorism involves terrorist acts that entail the citizens of the same country (Campbell, 2012). The risk associated with attacking Iraq was the chance of being attacked internally by citizens of the United States who sympathized with international domestic terrorists. Another risk could be additional attacks by international terrorists against the country. Therefore, prospect theory can also be presented as the "theory of risky choice" (Levy, 2012). The theory is considered risky as it uses gains and losses to determine how the decisions are made. As indicated earlier, the decisions made are based upon the judgments that have been assessed. In addition, the theory is also considered to be an inductive process. Prospect theory will allow a state to look at an agent to assess the risk, including gains and losses based on the decisions made (Campbell, 2012). It is important to note that the first three concepts of prospect theory spill over into the next three concepts.

The fourth concept of prospect theory exists in relation to behavior. Prospect theory is also perceived by scholars as a behavioral decision process. "The specific behaviors pertain to decision making under risk" (Campbell, 2012). Prospect theory attempts to predict how decisions are made. Therefore, the theory also focuses on behavior. A popular example of prospect theory and behavior is the study of consumers. Consumers are amongst the most highly measured group by the retail industry. Prospect theory is used to determine how consumers react and what types of behavior are attracted to high end expenditures. Prospect theory is used as a marketing tool to determine how messages should be framed. Also, prospect theory is used as a decision making tool to determine how to position and price a product in relation to consumer behavior (Cochran, 2001). Within the international economic system, prospect theory is quite popular.

In addition to international economies, prospect theory is also used to study the behaviors of terrorists. Terrorist behaviors are almost unpredictable. Suicide bombers for example, have amongst the most unpredictable forms of behavior. However, prospect theory can be used to negotiate with suicide bombers to deter them from pulling the trigger. The gains of negotiation with a suicide bomber can be predicted with the use of psychological manipulation to deter them from killing other innocent people within the surrounding area. The losses could be extensive, especially if the suicide bomber decides to pull the trigger, then several innocent people can be expected to die (McDermott, 2009). Prospect theory can also be used by governments and institutions to determine how to create a strategic plan for attacking a terrorist cell. It is important to note that terrorist cells are used in reference to terrorist groups. Terrorist cells exist all over the world today and seem to grow daily. However, the strategy to determine their next course of attack can be decided through evidence collected by special units' organization. Such information would be vital to further assist with assessing whether or not government institutions should attack a large and powerful terrorist group.

For example, the prospect theory may have been used by the CIA to plan the death of Osama Bin Laden. Bin Laden was killed in 2011 when CIA agents attacked him. However, it was a silent attack and unexpected that occurred during the early hours of the morning. The gains and losses were weighed heavily. The risk associated with this type of operation was extremely high. The risk was high because if the operation failed, then the entire world would know that the United States was trying to kill the most powerful and influential terrorist (Carroll, 2011). Therefore, the attacks against the United States and its allies would be expected by several terrorist cells. In addition, the risk associated with this operation was the danger of losing powerful CIA agents, as they too could have been killed. However, the operation was successfully completed as Bin Laden was killed according to the plan. Nevertheless, the gains included dismantling of Al Qaeda, the terrorist organization founded by Bin Laden. Also, the success of the operation resulted with a strong message to all terrorist cells. The message stated that no one powerful terrorist group could fight against the United States and win. Therefore, the prospect theory could have been used to determine the risk. Once the gains and losses were determined, a decision was made to move forward with the operation (Campbell, 2012).

Furthermore, prospect theory is established upon reference dependence. Reference dependence is the fifth concept of prospect theory. Reference dependence is the ability to make a decision that is contingent to a reference or standard (Campbell, 2012). The reference can be contingent to the status quo. Reference dependence also emphasizes the degree of changes in assets that pertain to gains and losses. The gains and losses are determined based on a single reference point. This single point will also be used to make the decision or choice. The choice or decision will be contingent upon seeking risk or risk aversion.

In addition, the final concept of prospect theory is the ability for individuals to respond to risk differently. Campbell (2012) states that individuals tend to overvalue losses in comparison to gains. Risk seeking occurs when individuals or organizations are given a choice to select one of the two options that may be presented. Risk seeking includes having the ability to achieve a certain value that could possibly provide gains. On the contrary, risk averse is a state of affairs that exists that encourages an individual to not take a risk. To better understand the notion of risk seeking and risk averse, the following example will be provided.

Please see Appendix A for a detailed diagram of risk seeking. Appendix A includes two charts that present the options of gaining money. Option A represents risk seeking and option B represents risk averse. Both options will be given to an individual who has the ability to gain a certain value. In option A, there is a seventy percent chance that an individual could gain five billion Euros. However, there exists a twenty five percent chance that no money could be gained. In option B, there is a one hundred percent chance that the individual could gain three billion Euros. However, there exists that if the latter option is selected, and nothing is won, then there is a chance that the individual can lose two billion Euros (Campbell, 2012). It is important to note that the loss was calculated by subtracting the five billion Euros from option A to the three billion Euros in option B.

The likelihood of gaining any additional money would be greater if option A was selected. Also, if option A is selected, then the individual has at least a seventy five percent chance of gaining five billion Euros versus only three billion Euros as presented in option B

(Campbell, 2012). It is important to note the majority of individuals or eighty percent of the population would select option B. The majority would select option B as there is a one hundred percent chance of gaining three billion Euros. The latter decision is known as risk averse. On the contrary, individuals who select option A would be referred to as risk seeking. Risk seekers would identify that their odds of gaining more money are higher if option A is selected (Campbell, 2012).

In relation to gains, individuals become more risk averse as they fear loss. However, the opposite is true for losses. Please see Appendix B that includes two charts which represent the options of losing money. The first chart labeled risk averse includes information related to option C. Option C states that an individual has a one hundred percent chance to lose three billion Euros immediately. Option D states that there exists a seventy five percent chance to lose fifteen billion Euros (Campbell, 2012). It also includes that there exists a twenty five percent chance to lose nothing at all. In such a situation, eighty percent of individuals would choose to take a risk. Twenty percent of individuals would be risk averse. Therefore, most individuals are more likely to select option D and seek risk. This further explains that individuals will become risk seekers at the time they have to confront a loss (Campbell, 2012). In international war and terrorism, risks are assessed similarly. However, the situation may vary depending on the type of conflict.

In addition to the concepts presented earlier, the findings of prospect theory are also vital to acknowledge as they are key components of this ideology. Levy (2000) presents six findings of prospect theory. The first finding illustrates that individuals' place value on things that they own rather than what they do not have. For example, in relation to international war and terror, it is expected to determine that individuals such as presidents, prime ministers and so on will become possessive of nuclear items that they own and belong to their nations. On an individual level, human beings will be very possessive of the items that they own, including homes, material possessions, and so on. Individuals however, will not be possessive of material items that they do not own or possess.

Furthermore, the second concept of the findings of prospect theory is the endowment effect. The endowment effect states that it is challenging to lose something rather gain it (Campbell, 2012). The difficultly with the loss is harder to accept as it can be very traumatic. Therefore, any additional gains that may be associated with this loss are not quickly accepted. For example, in relation to international war and terrorism, terrorists believe that their actions are not terrorist related. Their need to use violence such as bombings, kidnappings, and hijackings against the enemy are justified to result in victory. In addition, since terrorists also lack in funds to obtain weapons, or receive military support, they will use any form of target to obtain their victory with any available weaponry. This will also include the use of human lives to conduct suicide bombings. Innocent lives will be lost with suicide bombings, hijackings, and so on. However, terrorists realize that their gains are less than achieved when their loss becomes higher (Foley, n.d.).

The need to engage in such forms of violence is to achieve contact with political dignitaries. Nevertheless, political dignitaries will not provide them with the time or attention to negotiate. The loss of attention and negotiation for the terrorists is much more difficult to deal with as they will not receive any recognition to negotiate. Therefore, this loss will be difficult to comprehend by the terrorists, and as a result, will misperceive the political situation. Consequently, the loss of not being able to engage with the politicians will also result in hostility for the terrorist, who will continue to use violence to gain that attention. The time loss will be traumatic. Any gains associated with the loss time will reluctantly accepted (Foley, n.d.).

For instance, the 9/11 attacks in the United States conducted by Osama Bin Laden was executed on the basis of sending a message to the United States to remove their soldiers off of Saudi soil. The United States has aligned with Saudi Arabia for several years in hopes of having control of the oil. It is important to note that Osama Bin Laden was of Saudi origin and came with a personal wealth of three hundred million dollars. However, Bin Laden's wealth cannot be compared to the billions of dollars that the United States spends to send their troops overseas for the purpose of obtaining this oil. The desperate need for Bin Laden to gain the attention of the United States was to attack the major public points within the nation.

Although several thousand innocent lives were lost, the fact of the matter is that Bin Laden was willing to continue the perilous behavior to bring the status quo up to his reference point. It is important to note that his reference point was the need to remove U.S. troops out of Saudi soil. His loss was not only the money he spent conducting the operation, but the loss of days of U.S. troops on Saudi soil. The U.S. troops as soldiers continued to remain on the land despite the attacks at home. The latter was a more difficult loss for Bin Laden than the partial success of the 9/11 attacks (Foley, n.d.).

Also, risk orientation is another finding of prospect theory. Risk orientation assumes that there is a gain associated with risk averse than risk seeking in relation to losses. For example, individuals will take less of a risk when their chances are higher for gains (Campbell, 2012). The prisoner's dilemma is an example of risk orientation. In relation to international war and terror, "a prisoners' dilemma is a game of conflict in which the reward for unilateral noncooperation exceeds both benefit for mutual cooperation and cost of mutual conflict," (Foley, n.d.). In other words, with this game, if both players cooperate, then they both win. However, the opposite will hold true if both players have the desire to defect. The prisoner's dilemma is a tit for tat strategy.

A tit for tat strategy occurs when one player makes a specific move, and the opposition imitates the same move. To achieve a positive end result, both players will need to accept the terms of the strategy. For a negative outcome, if the second player defects, then the first player will also defect (Foley, n.d.). For example, if a terrorist group attacks the United States, then the likelihood of the nation attacking the terrorist group may be just as high.

In relation the prospect theory findings, the framing effect is also another key concept. The effect is the result of a change in a choice as a consequence of a change in the frame (Campbell, 2012). For example, in 2003 the United States attacked Iraq in hopes of combating terrorism. However, the decision to go to war was framed on the ability for the United States to expect losses, but achieve gains that would result in domestic gains for President Bush. In other words, the loss of lives would be high, along with the high expenditure of going to war.

However, if the United States succeeded in the war, the gains for the President would be higher. The President would receive favorable domestic support and encouragement from both the citizens and Congress. In addition, the largest gain would be for the United States to have access to foreign oil at its disposal. The risks outweighed the losses for this war. The war was framed with the notion to win. However, the outcome of the war did change the frame. The outcome of the war included the loss of high number of U.S. soldiers, including excess amounts of expenditure lost (Council on Foreign Relations, 2012). The prospect theory further increased the prospective that the President's decision to go to war was risk seeking in the domain of losses (Levy, 2000).

In addition, the fifth finding states that a reference point is not always fixed (Campbell, 2012). A reference point is set with the state of affairs. When a loss occurs with this state of affairs, then loss is difficult to endure. However, if there are additional gains from the loss of the state of affairs, the gains are even harder to accept. The latter is true as the individual will reflect on the initial loss. This is known as the endowment effect.

The endowment effect is the final finding of prospect theory. Campbell (2012) states that after gains are achieved faster than losses, there exists renormalization. Renormalization is the reorientation of a reference point. For example, after a series of continuous losses, it becomes difficult to adjust to any new gains. The latter holds true as individuals may frame the new situation based on an on old reference point. Therefore, any improvements could still be perceived as a loss. The individual may as a result, become a risk seeker in hopes to eliminate any losses to revisit the reference point (Campbell, 2012).

The findings of prospect theory provided an insight into the possible situations and outcomes of the ideology. In addition, there are two phases of prospect theory including, the editing phase, and the evaluation phase. The editing phase encompasses the judgments or assessments of the options, outcomes, and valuations (Campbell, 2012). The options are determined based on the outcomes. Once the decisions are made, the outcomes that occur are predicted in relation to prospect theory. The outcomes are then evaluated.

The evaluation phase weighs the outcomes against probabilities. Prior to a predicting an outcome, all situations must be weighed to determine the outcome. For example, the weight of risk averse for gains will be measured against risk seekers and losses (Campbell, 2012). For instance, prior to entering Iraq in 2003, the United States must have determined that eighty percent of the outcome of the war will be based on risk aversion with respect to gains. However, twenty percent of the outcome will be based on risk seeking with respect to loss. Since the predicted outcome of the war was eighty percent, the decision to move forward was made. Please note that this is a hypothetical example and does not reflect on any statistics regarding the war.

Both phases must predict the outcomes based upon the options. Thereafter, the outcomes will need to be evaluated to determine the percentage of gains or losses.

Prospect theory is a difficult ideology to apply to international relations and war. The theory has been created to seek individual related options and outcomes. Consumer behaviors toward the retail and food industry generally use prospect theory to understand the behavior of consumers. Therefore, attempting to apply prospect theory to international relations becomes rather difficult (Campbell, 2012). In addition, the concept of the endowment effect or renormalization is also a difficult concept to understand in relation to international war and terror. The gains and losses are also challenging to determine at the international level in comparison to the individual levels. In international war and terror, the risk assessment is based on collective group thinking. At the individual level, it is quite the opposite (Campbell, 2012). Therefore, to apply certain concepts of the prospect theory becomes very challenging due to the conditions associated with the international system.

Furthermore, prospect theory also becomes challenging to apply at the state level implications. States attempt to preserve the current state of affairs by remaining conservative with their spending and habits. However, with territorial defense, states will have to spend the money to protect their borders. They will further attempt to preserve the current state of affairs of their security within the international system. As a result, states will continue to frame their strategy of security to remain defensive. However, framing above or below the status quo can lead to unexpected gains or losses. If states frame above the current state of affairs, then the status quo may be perceived as a loss. The opposite holds true for frames below the status quo that could result in gains (Campbell, 2012).

However, with the concept of reorientation of the reference point, states do not desire a decline in relative power. Therefore, states that lose power or have a loss will attempt to encroach what they have lost against another state. For example, Levy (2000) states that if state A wins land from State B, then State B will attempt to encroach its loss from State A by seeking risk. It will take a risk in an attempt to return to its normal reference point. Nevertheless, State A will enjoy the benefits of its gains and attempt to maintain its new state of affairs. This will likely hold true with international war and terror, but the scenario will not be so simple. In fact, when states attempt to take territories that they do not previously own, it becomes a destructive situation, where neither party will gain anything substantial. It may result in a deadlock or non agreement (Campbell, 2012). Prospect theory is a difficult theory to use with international war and terror. The predictions are not always achievable as information is difficult to obtain from either party. However, prospect theory is a possible ideology that can be used to predict the behavior of other states and parties in hopes of achieving power.

This paper presented the concepts and findings of prospect theory. Also, this paper illustrated the phases of prospect theory in relation to international war and terrorism. The ideology is an inductive process that seeks to determine how decisions should be based against weighted options. Outcomes are always difficult to determine. However, with the study of behavior of other states and parties, prospect theory can be used to make vital decisions. The decisions will ultimately present the actual outcomes, which need to be evaluated. To combat terroristic behavior such as suicide bombings, prospect theory can be a useful tool. The behavior of suicide bombers can be used to predict their actions. Nations can create strategies to combat suicide bombers through the study of their behavior. However, the need to apply prospect theory in all events related to international war and terror has yet to be proven useful.

References

Campbell, J. (2012). *International War & Terrorism.* Retrieved on May 16, 2012 to May 30,

    2012 from, http://www.youtube.com/view_play_list?p=B5FFE60CFDB74A00

Carroll, W. (2011). *Osama Bin Laden is Dead.* Retrieved on June 12, 2012 from,

    http://www.military.com/news/article/osama-bin-laden-killed.html

Chapple, I. (2012). *Spain in eurozone crisis crosshairs.* Retrieved on June 11, 2012 from,

    http://www.cnn.com/2012/06/07/business/spain-euro-crisis/index.html?hpt=wo_c2

Cochran, A. (2001). *Prospect Theory & Customer Choice.* Retrieved on June 11, 2012 from,

Council on Foreign Relations. (2012). *Timeline: The Iraq War.* Retrieved on June 14, 2012 from,

    http://www.cfr.org/iraq/timeline-iraq-

    war/p18876?gclid=CL7l7pipzrACFYeR7Qod0wOKMA

Foley, T. (n.d.). *Countering the Terrorist Threat.* Retrieved June 14, 2012 from, http://www-

    personal.umich.edu/~rtanter/F98PS472PAPERS/FOLEY.TIM.FREELANCE.HTML

Levy, J. (2000). "Perspectives from Prospect Theory in in Midlarsky, ed. *Handbook of War*

    Studies II. 2000. University of Michigan Press. Pg., 193-221.

McDermott, R. (2009). *Prospect Theory and Negotiation.* Retrieved on June 11, 2012 from,

    https://springerlink3.metapress.com/content/lh3543780t557434/resource-

    secured/?target=fulltext.pdf&sid=yupwp3s3zahasbeivwo1fe3p&sh=www.springerlink.co

    m

White, D. (2012). *Iraq War Facts, Results & Statistics at January 31, 2012.* Retrieved article on

    June 11, 2012 from http://usliberals.about.com/od/homelandsecurit1/a/IraqNumbers.htm

Appendix A: Gains

Option A: Risk Seeking

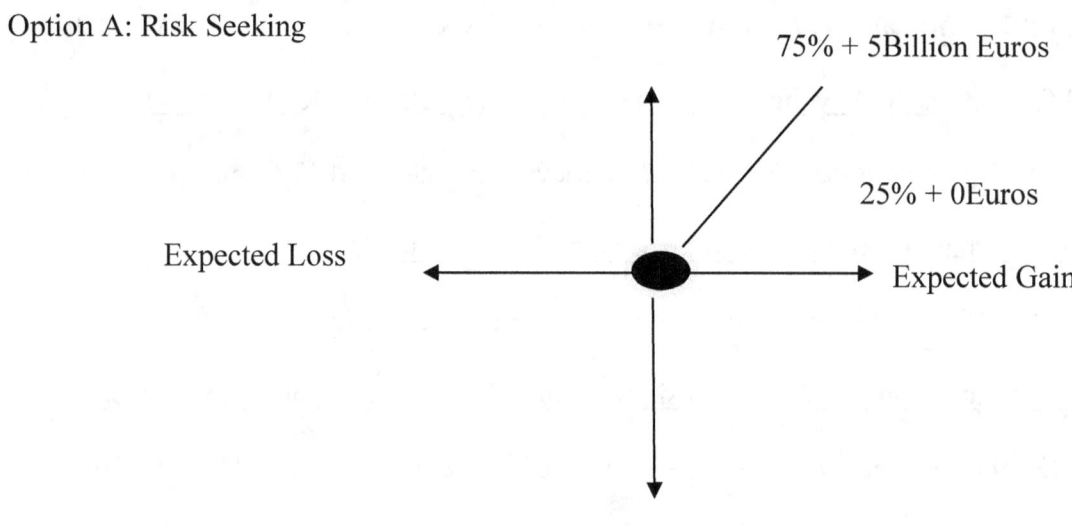

75% + 5Billion Euros

25% + 0Euros

Expected Loss

Expected Gain

Certain Loss

Option B: Risk Averse

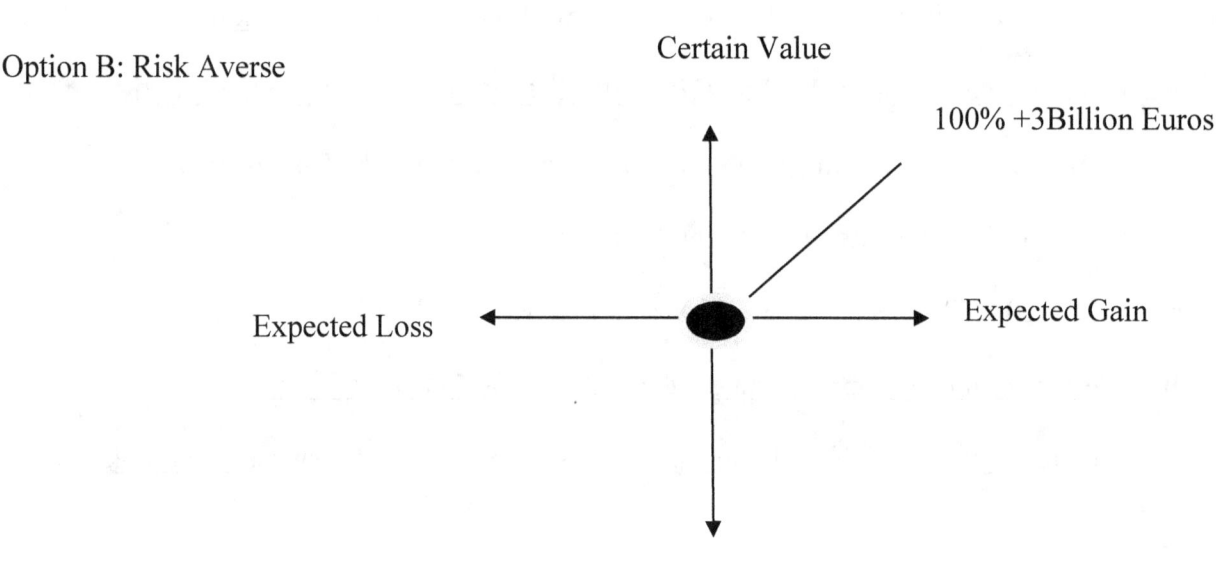

Certain Value

100% +3Billion Euros

Expected Loss

Expected Gain

Certain Loss

(Campbell, 2012).

Appendix B: Losses

Option C: Risk Averse

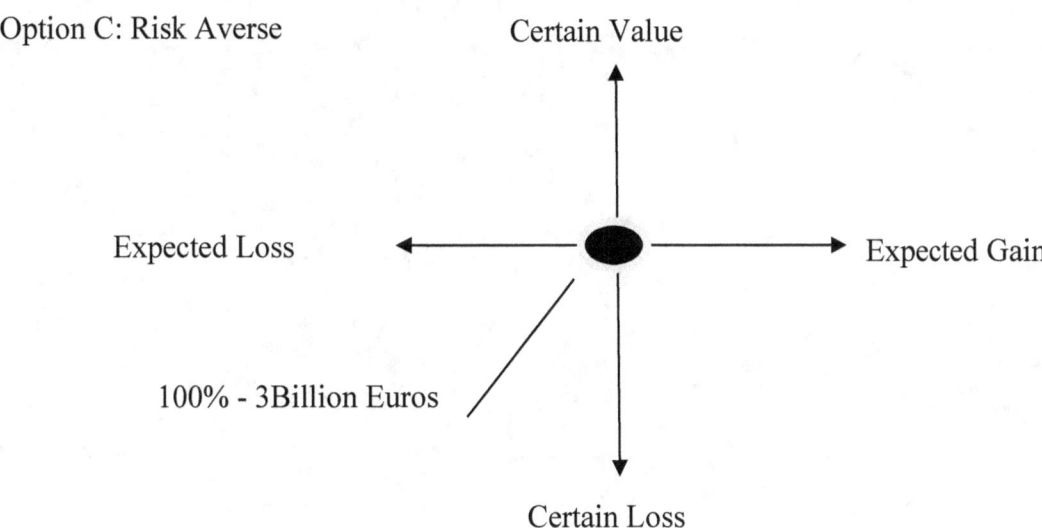

Option D: Risk Seeking

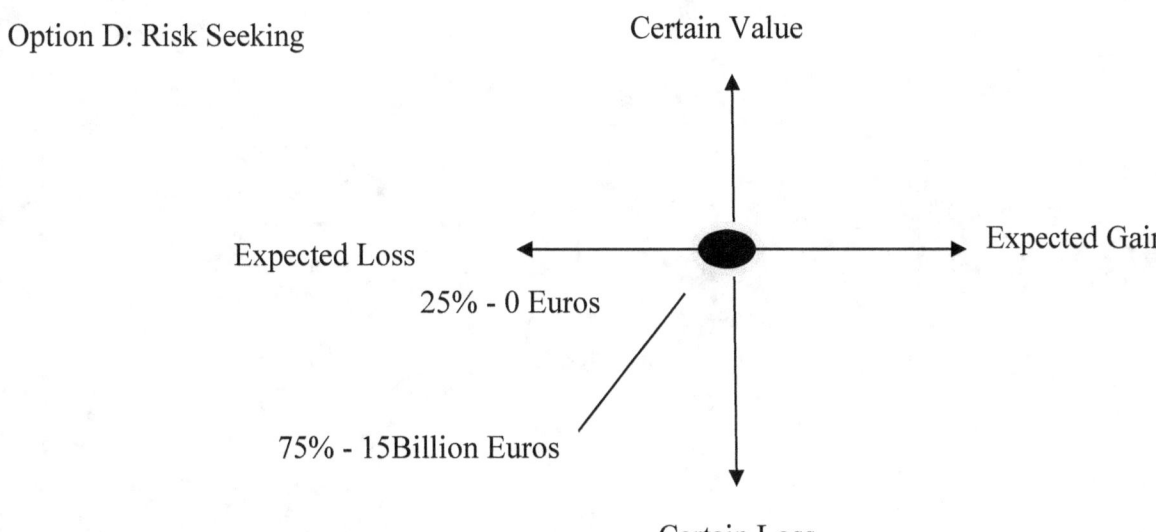

(Campbell, 2012).

Cyber Security: Nature, Dimensions and Threats Facing Bangladesh

Ishtiaque Alam

Abstract

The advancement of information and technology has ushered a revolution in the field of communication, development and security. Internet has unlocked the unending potential of collaboration and cooperation. But it has, at the same time, brought risks of an unprecedented asymmetric nature. Cyber threats are now regarded as an asymmetric weapon of warfare and it is also regarded as the fifth domain where war can be waged. This paper has examined the perils and pitfalls associate with cyber threats and draws attention to Bangladesh. It has discussed the cyber-attacks carried out in Bangladesh and critically analyzed the prevailing countermeasures and their weaknesses. Finally, in order to face upcoming challenges of the future, the paper has put forward some recommendations for better cyberspace security management in the context of Bangladesh.

Introduction

Cyber security has become a serious concern for the policy makers. With the swift advancement of globalization concerns have emerged on how to tackle the threats posed by the cyberspace. Governments are increasingly allocating resources to this particular domain. Bush Administration, for instance, began development of a *Comprehensive National Cybersecurity Initiative (CNCI)* in January 2008. The Obama Administration has followed with a *Cyberspace Policy Review* and a promised to appoint a "Cyber Czar" to coordinate the federal government's response. Threats arising from cyberspace are various in kinds and nature. Computers are instrumental in the day-to-day operations of companies, organizations, and governments. Companies large and small rely on computers to manage payroll, to track inventory and sales, and to perform research and development. Distribution of necessities from producers to retail customers relies on computers and networks at every stage. Nearly everyone in business or government relies on electronic communications; telephone, fax, e-mail, or instant messages – which are enabled by computers. Breach of any of these networks would disrupt all systems that rely on internet.

The world is vulnerable to attacks from cyber terrorists. The cyber terrorists are cunning and willing to use any weakness to their advantage. To quote Muhammad Atef, the former military commander of Al-Qaeda, and Ayman Muhammad Rabi' al-Zawahiri, founder of the Egyptian terrorist group, Islamic Jihad, who became a close, influential confidant of bin Laden:

"Divide their nation, tear them to shreds, destroy their economy, burn their companies, ruin their welfare, sink their ships and kill them on land, sea and air. Your dependence on technology makes you weak. More brothers await orders to attack again. They will attack your powerful

companies, like Microsoft, from the inside and you will not know when or how. Through these attacks your power will fail, your communications will fail, your businesses will starve, your economy will crumble, your people will panic, your military and firemen will be immobilized, and God willing, you will one day be incapable of sustaining the sinful deployment of your infidel army throughout the land of the two holy places."[i]

The technological advancements have actually made technologically dependent countries more vulnerable to disruption. Physical security is now permanently tied to cyber security. While not "mass destructive," attacks on critical infrastructure would certainly be "mass disruptive."[ii] Hence, cyber security has become an utmost concern for not only governments but also individual corporations and individual beings.

Understanding cyber threat

"To fight and conquer in all your battles is not supreme excellence; supreme excellence consists in breaking the enemy's resistance without fighting."

-Sun Tzu

Cyber threats are challenges that are posed to almost all the sectors of globalized world. Cyber threat is defined broadly as any threat that uses a computer network in any phase of the threats.[iii] Cyberspace – the global digital communication and information transfer infrastructure – presents a wide range of security challenges for private individuals, commercial enterprises, governments and international organizations. These challenges, usually grouped under the term cyber security. Cyber-attacks enable a party to engage its opponent without face it directly. Here the above ancient dictum of Sun Tzu's famous masterpiece on strategy the "Art of War" is very pertinent. It also keeps an option open to withdraw from the scene without a trace. Cyber threats are any internet borne activity that may harm or have the potential to harm a computer or network and compromises the confidentiality, integrity, or availability of network data or systems.

According to Merriam Webster dictionary "cyber security is measures taken to protect a computer or computer system (as on the Internet) against unauthorized access or attack".[iv] Joe Weiss, a photojournalist and multimedia reporter, has attributed to cyber threats as "an occurrence that actually or potentially jeopardizes the confidentiality, integrity, or availability of an information system or that constitutes a violation or imminent threat of violation of security policies, security procedures, or acceptable use policies. Incidents may be intentional or unintentional."[v] Cyber-attack, on the other hand, disrupts the integrity or authenticity of data, usually through malicious code that alters program logic that controls data, leading to output errors.

Motives of cyber threat

Every action is driven by some purpose. Cyber attackers and cyber criminals are no exception. Even technical curiosity is attributed to challenge of capacity. As Internet usage continues to rise throughout the world, the threat of cybercrime also grows. While some of these crimes are relatively harmless and commonplace, others are very serious. Some of the motives of cyber threats are:

1. **Hacking as technical curiosity**

Recreational hackers may appear relatively benign. Many are attracted by the challenge of gaining access to a system and showing up failings in the company's security. But they can still cause damage that result in a financial loss for their victims. Major motives for hacking are monetary gain; testing computer security; intellectual challenge; power; self-expression and peer recognition; youth frivolity, mischief or curiosity. In other words hacking motives may summarize as MEECES which stands for money, entertainment, ego, cause, entrance to social groups and status.[vi] There are some who hack for personal pleasure. The launching of the Morris worm, which partially disabled the Internet, is an example of the result of curiosity leading to unexpected consequences.[vii]

2. Profit motive

Criminal-minded hackers' motives include financial gain, sabotage or revenge. In 1994, the US Citibank was robbed of $400,000 by Russian cyber-criminals. The theft of confidential information from companies may also be used for blackmail. Hackers also carry out espionage and sabotage. Political hackers - sometimes called "Hacktivists" - deface web sites in an attempt to put across their message and discredit their opponents. In 1998, hackers altered hundreds of web sites around the world to include an anti-nuclear message. There has been a convergence of hacking activity performed for monetary gain:

- Hackers sell email lists to spammers who create backdoors using Trojan horses, infected computers may then be made available as part of a 'bot army' to launch denial of service attacks enabling extortion (online betting services).

- In the United States, an employee of AOL has been charged with stealing the email subscriber list and selling it to a spammer who then sold it to others.

3. Breaching national security

Although direct cyber-attack against national security infrastructure is rare but a growing concern is generating on terrorist attack on national security architecture. It is increasingly being recognized that web-based activity is used to finance terrorism. Hacking has the capacity to cause damage, or aggravate damage from other forms of attack. Items that are critical to the national information infrastructure or key utilities involving energy, communication, health and hazardous materials provide obvious targets for malicious hacking.

It is known that many Al-Qaeda members are well educated, and have familiarity with engineering and other technical areas. In 2006 it was reported that an organization linked to Al-Qaeda produced a 26-page manual providing instructions on the use of the Google search engine to further the goals of global jihad. Recently British forces in Iraq have found print-outs of Google-Earth pictures that reportedly were to be used for targeting of coalition forces.[viii] *The Washington Times* has reported that Islamic extremists are calling for creation of an Islamist hackers' army to plan cyber-attacks against the U.S. government.[ix]

Objectives of cyber security

The strategic objectives of securing cyberspace are to prevent cyber-attacks against a state's critical infrastructures, reduce national vulnerability to cyber-attacks, and minimize damage and recovery time from cyber-attacks. Virtually every type of government services are now depends on cyberspace. Governments at all levels perform essential services in the agriculture; food; water; public-health; emergency-services; defense; social-welfare; information and telecommunications; energy; transportation; banking and finance; chemicals; and postal and shipping sectors that depend upon cyberspace for their delivery. As such, the major aims of cyber security are:

1. Ensure continuity of services

The very objective of cyber security is to help government agencies and private organizations to meet information security needs by ensuring continuity of critical services. Enabling secure communication and collaboration, supporting regulatory compliance, and creating public-private architecture are the major aims of cyber protection. The endeavor of cyber security is to ensure government agencies' network-infrastructure availability and continuity of government services.

2. Communicate and collaborate freely

Unfettered data sharing, communication, and collaboration require not only reliable security mechanisms but also easy interoperability with applications and devices, regardless of platform or environment. The popularity of internet is so high just because it enables people to maintain instant communication and generously cooperate with each other. Cyber-attack can standstill activities what is considered "daily" activities online. Online collaboration and financial transactions will face danger in the event of a cyber-attack. It has always been one of the most important priorities of cyber security to maintain a secure and smooth communication and collaboration pathways for ceaseless interaction.

3. Reduce cost through public-private engagement

Nearly every facet of modern life is connected to the internet and the associated wireless environment in some way. Individuals, businesses and government organizations, are all at risk to the prolific threats impacting on online networks. The lack of coordination between public and private sector leaves the user vulnerable to malicious behavior that, among a long list of possibilities, can invade their privacy, steal their identities, deny critical services, or create conditions in which public confidence in governmental institutions is diminished. Cyberspace security is a matter of vast responsibility. Neither a single government nor an individual organization has the capacity of maintain a safe cyberspace without any malicious threat emanating from it. It is not possible for a government to check and maintain every mile cyber optic cable for smooth functioning. Not every cyber infrastructure is owned by government in every country and that brings the urgency of a public-private partnership to secure the critical cyber infrastructure.

An effective public-private partnership for cyber security would provide the abilities to detect threats to create more secure network environments through better, standardized security programs and protocols and to respond with warnings or technical fixes as needed. It is crucial to address the vulnerabilities of cyberspace in a systematic manner, through a partnership of all stakeholders.

4. National security safeguarding

Howard Schmidt, Special advisor for Cyber Security in the White House, opined that:

"There is a very real and growing threat to national security that can no longer be ignored and viewed as just a government problem. Instead of waiting with bated breath for the next high-profile attack, CIOs and IT directors everywhere must prepare for every possible eventuality."[x]

Several countries are facing hostile and insistent attacks against critical government computer systems that hold military and national security secrets, confidential federal documents and personal data including social security numbers, medical and tax records. Even, the e-mails, of Defense Secretary Robert Gates, have been infiltrated and classified data were stolen from the Pentagon's most technologically advanced fighter aircraft, and State Department computers and the electrical grids were hacked.

Various national security matters are related to cyberspace. Weapons development, classified data transfer, financial transaction of different banks etc. are related to national security concerns. Vulnerabilities like hacking, denial of services; cyber stalking could endanger national security secrets. Terrorists or hackers could cause financial chaos by tampering with Wall Street's computerized trading system. Cyberspace has come to the forefront of modern security attention. Cyberspace has indeed become the fifth domain of warfare after land, sea, air and space. Even President Obama has declared America's digital infrastructure to be a "strategic national asset".[xi] Cyberspace certainly will be part of any future war. Potential enemies are no longer on the other side of the ocean, but just behind the firewall. In the words of Steven Chabinsky, a senior FBI official responsible for cyber security that "given enough time, motivation and funding, a determined adversary will always—always—be able to penetrate a targeted system."[xii] Cyber weapons are developed not just because of causing destruction but to disrupt and slow down potential opponents. Hence, preserving national security information infrastructure is undoubtedly a prime concern for cyber security.

5. Safety of critical infrastructure

Cyber security entails the safeguarding of computer networks and the information they contain from penetration and disruption. Since the use of computer networks has become a major element in governmental and business activities, tampering with these networks can have serious consequences for agencies, firms and individuals. Potential opponents may include conventional nation-state opponents and "non-state actors." Cyber weapons are considered attractive for asymmetric attacks because they could offer low-cost means of exploiting the potentially damaging vulnerabilities that are found in most computer networks. Some analysts go further and argue that a cyber-weapon could create destruction equal to a kinetic or blast weapon, or could amplify the effects of an attack with these kinds of weapons.

The security of critical infrastructure arises from the apprehension that a more sophisticated opponent will not use network attacks in an attempt to cause physical damage or terror, but instead target the information stored within computer networks. Nation-states are likely to be attracted to this approach: penetrate networks, collect information and observe activities without arousing suspicion and, should a conflict begin, use that access to disrupt databases and networks that support key activities. Secretary of Homeland Security of the United States gave priority to efforts that would reduce risk in "critical infrastructure and key resources that could be exploited to cause catastrophic health effects or mass casualties comparable to those from the use of a weapon of mass destruction."[xiii] There are a few networks that are national in scope and interconnect thousands of entities in ways that make them mutually dependent. However, these networks—finance, telecommunications, electrical power—are among the most critical for national security and economic health, and their interconnectedness, national scope and criticality may make them more attractive targets for cyber-attack. There have been thousands of hacking incidents aimed at power companies.[xiv] The internet itself is a single large infrastructure that could be attacked with cyber weapons. The first point to bear in mind, however, is that it is a shared global network. An attack against it will affect both target and attacker. There has been at least one effort to attack the internet in the United States. An October 2002 attack by unknown parties used a Distributed Denial of Service attack against the 13 "root servers" that govern internet addresses. The attacks forced eight of the thirteen servers off-line.

It may be more accurate to say that critical infrastructures are dependent on their human operators, whose actions are supported, reinforced or carried out using computers and networks. This human element reduces the risk of cyber-attack to critical infrastructures. Nonetheless, it is the infrastructure which performs the ultimate tasks and any threat to its functioning obviously affects the overall performance. Therefore, safety of critical infrastructure from cyber threat will always remain a principal matter of concern.

Why cyber-attack on critical infrastructure?

"History teaches us that in asymmetric warfare the most heavily armed do not always win."

-Ignacio Ramonet[xv]

Modern societies are so interconnected with each and every other system that any disturbance in these systems could bring a high degree of chaos. As a reminder of how dependent society is on its infrastructure, in May 1998, PanAmSat's Galaxy IV satellite's on-board controller malfunctioned, disrupting service to an estimated 80-90% of the USA's pagers, causing problems for hospitals trying to reach doctors on call, emergency workers, and people trying to use their credit cards at gas pumps, to name but a few.

In both developing and developed countries critical infrastructure is connected to the internet and can lack proper security precautions, leaving these installations vulnerable to attacks. The whole purpose of a cyber-attack is to cause some sort of adverse impact on whatever the perpetrator is targeting. Without the appropriate protection combined with the current lack of preparedness, an attack on these infrastructures would be detrimental and will cause more destruction than any previous cyber-attacks. Major critical infrastructures are electricity generation; transmission and distribution; gas production, transport, and distribution; oil and oil products production, transport and distribution; telecommunication; water supply (drinking water, waste water/sewage, and stemming of surface water); public health (hospitals, ambulances); transportation systems (fuel supply, railway network, airports, harbors) and financial services (banking, clearing) etc.

Apart from cost, the most widely feared loss from attacks is damage to reputation, followed by the loss of personal information of customers. For this reason alone, most cases of critical infrastructure cyber-attacks remain unreported.

Cyber weapons can cause national security breaches. Military installations are vulnerable because they rely on electric grid. In the case of any attack of nation's infrastructure it will pound upon the national psyche. Financially motivated attacks like extortion and theft-of-service are widespread. The economic impacts of cyber-attacks are also mounting. The reported cost of downtime from major attacks exceeds US$6 million per day, but in some sectors such as oil and gas it can surpass US$8 million per day. Besides the loss of life, the terrorist attacks of September 11 disrupted the services of a number of critical infrastructures including telecommunications, the internet, financial markets, and air transportation. The cost physical protection of critical infrastructure is also gigantic. The Bush Administration estimated that it requested $2.6 billion for critical infrastructure protection for FY2002. The reason why Bush administration is spending increasing amount of fund for infrastructure protection is that collapsed infrastructure enhances the possibility of physical attacks. Nonetheless, cyber criminals and hackers are now increasingly being recognized as asymmetric warriors and internet is now recognized as a tool of asymmetric warfare. Non-state actors do not face the same political constraints that apply to state actions in cyberspace. In theory, a non-state actor could hire cybercriminals to launch an attack that was beyond its own capabilities, and there is one media report that Israel suspects the Hamas or Hezbollah may have hired Russian cybercriminals for an attack against its networks. Thus the capabilities of non-state actors cannot and should not be neglected.

Internet: Bangladesh picture

Commercially internet comes into operation in the mid-1990s in Bangladesh. VSAT based data circuit was commissioned in Bangladesh in 1996. Just after one year in 1997, tremendous development was observed in the growth of internet in Bangladesh. Now the number of internet users and number of Internet Service Providers (ISP) are growing rapidly. According to International Telecommunication Union (ITU) presently the number of internet users in Bangladesh is 5,570,535 as of December, 2011, 3.5% of the population[xvi]. As of Bangladesh Telecommunication Regulatory Commission (BTRC) of Bangladesh March 2012 statistics, the number of mobile subscribers is just over 92 million and mobile internet access over 25 million users.[xvii] Telecommunication services are now more affordable in Bangladesh. To increase countrywide internet services via submarine cable, internet bandwidth price has been reduced by

33%. The number of mobile internet users is estimated to have risen by 30% in the past six months.[xviii]

Reported cyber-attacks in Bangladesh

Cybercrime is gaining ground in Bangladesh. The website of the Rapid Action Battalion (RAB) was hacked in 2008 by four students of a private technology institute.[xix] The hackers said that they hacked RAB's website just for adventure, while the RAB termed it a criminal act. Prior to this incident an e-mail was sent to Daily Star, a daily newspaper of Bangladesh, issuing a life threat to Sheikh Hasina, the then opposition leader. The e-mail reads:

"Hello Sheikh Hasina, this is Al-Kaeda Group from your surroundings. Very soon, you will be killed by Al-Kaeda Group wherever you are. We want to (know) you through this newspaper about your death process. Be ready in USA or in Bangladesh. Yours enemy, Al-Kaeda Group Dhaka, Bangladesh."[xx]

Another e-mail was sent to the police headquarter, threatening the then prime minister Khaleda Zia and her eldest son. Two young men, a private university student and a software engineer, were arrested in connection with the e-mail threatening the prime minister and another youth for threatening Sheikh Hasina. The first two have reportedly said that they had sent the mail for fun. As there is no nationwide computer infrastructure, no watchdog or security system has yet been developed in Bangladesh. RAB recently arrested JMB's IT chief Rajib, who confessed that he had downloaded information on explosives from the internet, translated them into Bengali and sent them to Mizan, JMB's explosive expert, who made explosives on the basis of this information.[xxi] Some years back, hackers inserted pornographies to the website of Bangladesh National parliament.[xxii]

A Dhaka-based Facebook stocks tipster, Mahbub Sarwar, was arrested on charges of illegally manipulating the Dhaka Stock Exchange. The police said that Mahbub's Facebook account has around 3,000 members and he has a number of blogs' and that they believe 'around 10,000 or more people have been acting on his tips for the last few months.'[xxiii] Police headquarters recently requested the Home Ministry to close down 84 websites, which have thousands of porno pictures on display and are provoking sexual crimes and violence.[xxiv] Popular social networking site Facebook had been temporarily banned in Bangladesh owing to criminal activities of a twenty-four year old male apprehended with the charge of faking identities of different people and of uploading defamatory images of several political personalities. "Cyber-crime and technology related crimes are on the rise and current trends indicate that it will be a significant issue in South and South-East Asia," said Additional Inspector General NBK Tripura in an interview. "We are aware that, in this modern day and age, crime is not bound by borders and takes advantage of the technology available on the market. We are preparing ourselves to fight hi-tech crime," Tripura said.[xxv]

Reported cyber attacks

2008	RAB website hacked.
October 2004	Sheikh Hasina threatened by an email.
August 2004	Khaleda Zia threatened by an email.
June 2009	JMB IT chief arrested.
2010	Prime minister's office controlled website hacked.
2010	Dhaka Stock Exchange manipulated through Facebook.
2010	Facebook banned due to uploading defamatory images of several political personalities.

Bangladesh "Information and Communication Technology Act 2006": Is it enough?

Bangladesh adopted an act on 8th October, 2006 named as "Information and Communication Technology Act, 2006"[xxvi] to provide the information and communication technology a legalized and secure platform. This Act governs over a good number of areas such as creating, sending and receiving of electronic mails or electronic records, issuance of electronic certificate and electronic license. This Act also deals with the authority which holds the power to adjudicate the offences under this act, the cyber offence, punishments, trial procedure, establishment of cyber appeal tribunal etc.

The significant cyber offences listed in the Act are:

Section 4: If someone commits a crime under the Act in any place outside Bangladesh, it shall be treated in the same way as if the offence has been committed in Bangladesh.

Section 54: Destruction of computer and computer system by-unauthorized access, collection, infiltration of computer virus in computer or network, destruction of storage mediums of a network, willful intervention in a network, assisting unauthorized personnel to enter into a network, sending SPAM or unwanted email to promote or sell any product without the permission of the client or the sender and depositing any person's payment for certain service in another account by illegal intervention or fraud.

Section 55: Concealing, altering or destructing source code in a computer, computer program or a computer network.

Section 56: by hacking into any computer or any computer system in an unauthorized way.

Section 57: According to section 57 (1), any person publishing or broadcasting any such material (text, pictorial or audiovisual) on website or any other electronic form which is falsified or vulgar, and upon reading, writing or listening to that material, any person (natural person, partnership business, company, statuary institution and cooperation society) becomes derailed or provoked or defamed or the law and order situation gets worsened or personal and state image is being harmed or anyone's religious feeling is in under attack or by providing these materials, provocation is instigated against any person or group of person; this very action is a punishable offence. Section 57 (2) briefs that anyone committing an offence under 57(1) will be punished with a sentence of imprisonment not more than 10 years and a fine not more than Tk. 10 million.

The legislation is not sufficient to effectively deal with cybercrimes. For, the offences under this act are non-cognizable. That is, the police shall not arrest the alleged offenders without a warrant of arrest. The non-cognoscibility of an offence may weaken the Act as it gives the perpetrators an upper hand over the victims.

Another important aspect is the recent upsurge of child pornography in Bangladesh. In Bangladesh the law that directly deals with pornography is 149 years old, and there is no wonder that it does not cover the Internet or Multi-media Messages. Section 292 of the Penal Code defines porn as "obscene book, pamphlet, paper, drawing, painting, representation or figure or any other obscene object whatsoever", and hands down prison sentences up to six months to a person who sells, lets to hire, distributes, exhibits or circulates to "any person under the age of twenty years". Section 292 does not even mention children, and lawyer Barrister Raghib Rauf Chowdhury, an eminent lawyer in Bangladesh, finds it poorly made to fight the rising menace of child pornography.[xxvii] The Children Act 1974 does not cover child pornography and the Act which does -- Information and Communications Technology (ICT) Act 2006; does not specifically mention any offence committed by or against the juveniles. "The ICT Act carries severe punishment with a prison sentence of up to 10 years and a fine of up to Tk. 10 million. But the law is not clear enough to cover the situation that we are dealing with nowadays," Barrister Chowdhury says.[xxviii] Reviewing the salient features of the Act, it seems more concerned for the television channels than the pornographers or owners of pornographic sites. The laws as well as the investigation procedure in Bangladesh relating to the cybercrimes are still in a very primary stage and are yet to be developed. As per the ICT Act, the government was supposed to establish a Cyber Tribunal to try the cases for violation of the provisions contained in the ICT Act. Regrettably, such specialized Cyber Tribunal has not yet been established.

Options and concluding thoughts

Analyzing the current trends and challenges posed by cyber threats, Bangladesh needs to consider a number of ways to mitigate the vulnerabilities. Some of them are:

1. Bangladesh, being a member of INTERPOL, may seek help to secure the punishment of net criminals regardless of territory using INTERPOL's global secure police communications system.

2. A special analysis site in conformity with global secure police communication system may also be developed which would provide real-time monitoring of cyber activities.

3. 'Cyber Incident Response Unit' and a 'Cyber Crime Investigation Cell' may be built with law enforcement mechanism to fight cybercrimes successfully.

4. Cyber counter intelligence team could prove very useful.

5. Training of officers to become experts in the field and providing adequate logistic support and equipment are of prime significance.

6. Web servers running public sites must be separately protected from internal corporate networks. Web site owners should watch and check any inconsistency on the site by installing host-based intrusion detection devices on servers.

7. Efforts need to be taken to collect and preserve statistics of cybercrimes and the monetary loss due to cyber criminality. Many countries have set up organizations like Computer Emergency Readiness Team (CERT) like USA, UK, India, Malaysia etc. Bangladesh should have one of its own.

8. Programs should be taken like national infrastructure protection and computer intrusion to continually assess the threat of computer crime.

9. Enactment of domestic laws can be proved very useful. Good news is Bangladesh has an "ICT Act" that can come very handy if properly enforced.

10. Global cooperation to fight cybercrime is the last step which Bangladesh should not overlook.

Bangladesh police recently has taken plan to set up a special unit to curb cybercrimes. The police department has decided to set up a cybercrime control unit, which will be the country's first policing unit against cybercrime. The police department trained some officers in 2007 to combat such hi-tech crimes.[xxix] The Bangladesh Police in association with the Australian Federal Police has organized training workshops on cybercrime with an aim to share experiences and foster cooperation in combating cybercrime.[xxx] Australian High Commissioner Douglas Foskett said 'cybercrime has become an issue of concern all over the world. As

Bangladesh is witnessing a rapid growth in the use of internet, it needs to prepare to face the threat.' Australian Hi-Tech Crime Centre is offering assistance to different countries in this regard. Microsoft Bangladesh had organized a training session for law enforcers and public sector officials on cybercrime fighting tactics under its *Security Cooperation Program* introduced in Bangladesh in 2007.[xxxi] Bangladesh adopted ICT Act, 2006 to provide the information and communication technology a legalized and secure platform. Bangladesh is trying to formulate a cybercrime law and a draft law is already in the hand.[xxxii] Finally, creating social awareness and developing a national consensus against cyber threats will prove to be a big step forward to face the challenges. Otherwise, the biggest possibilities which the cyberspace is providing would become its worst nightmares. Bangladesh's reliance on cyberspace will only grow in the years ahead. This national dependency must be managed with continuous efforts to secure cyber systems and the networks in order to protect the economy and secure national security. A well-articulated national strategy will be an indication of the nation's resolve to protect its cyberspace. The government needs to conduct a national dialogue[xxxiii] on cyber security to develop more public awareness about the threat and risks and to ensure an integrated approach toward the nation's need for security and the national commitment to privacy rights and civil liberties guaranteed by the constitution and law.

References

i Rohan Gunaratna, *Inside Al-Qaeda: Global Network of Terror* (New York: Berkley Books, 2003), p. 47

ii Vikky Spencer, "Cyber Terrorism: Mass Destruction or Mass Disruption?," available at: http://www.crime-research.org/eng/library/mi2g.htm (accessed on July 17, 2010).

iii N. Kshetri, "Pattern of global cyber war and crime: A Conceptual Framework," *Journal of International Management*, no. 11, pp. 540-562

4 http://www.merriam-webster.com/dictionary/cyber%20security (accessed on July 19, 2010).

v http://www.digitalbond.com/index.php/2010/08/03/how-should-we-treat-cyber-incidents/ (accessed on July 19, 2010).

vi "Hacking motives," *Hightech Crime Brief*, no. 6, Australian Institute of Criminology, available at: http://www.aic.gov.au/documents/1/B/A/%7B1BA0F612-613A-494D-B6C5-06938FE8BB53%7Dhtcb006.pdf (accessed on July 19, 2010).

vii P. Grabosky & R. Smith, *Crime in the digital age* (Sydney: Federation Press, 1998)

viii Thomas Harding, "Terrorists use Google Maps to hit UK Troops," *Telegraph*, 13 January, 2007, available at: http://www.telegraph.co.uk/news/main.jhtml?xml=/news/2007/01/13/ wgoogle13.xml] (accessed on July 21, 2010).

ix Shaun Waterman, "Islamists Seek To Organize Hackers' Jihad in Cyberspace," *Washington Times*, August 26, 2005, p. 9.

x "*Howard Schmidt on cyber threats to national security*," available at: http://www.net-security.org/secworld.php?id=5654 (accessed on July 21, 2010).

xi "War in the fifth domain," *The Economist*, July 3, 2010, p. 20.

xii Ibid, p. 21

xiii "Critical Infrastructure Identification, Prioritization, and Protection," December 17, 2003, available at http://www.whitehouse.gov/news/releases/2003/12/20031217-5.html (accessed on July 28, 2010).

xiv "Hackers Hit Power Companies," *CBS News*, July 8, 2002, available at http://www.cbsnews.com/stories/2002/07/08/tech/main514426.html (accessed on July 28, 2010).

xv Ignacio Ramonet, "Unjustified means," *Le Monde diplomaticque*, November 1, 2001, available at http://mondediplo.com/2001/11/01unjustified (accessed on August 2, 2010).

xvi http://www.internetworldstats.com/asia/bd.htm

xvii "Internet trends in Bangladesh" *The Daily Star*, July 13, 2012

xviii "'To do' for Digital Bangladesh," *The Daily Star*, March 4, 2010.

xix "RAB website hacked," *The Daily Star*, September 6, 2008.

xx "The Daily Star receives e-mail threatening to kill Hasina," *The Daily Star*, October 31, 2004.

xxi "JMB IT 'chief' captured," *The Daily Star*, June 23, 2009.

xxii "Cyber crime in 'Digital Bangladesh," *The Daily Star*, June 20, 2009.

xxiii http: //en.kioskea.net/news/ 15123-bangladesh-police-arrest-facebook-share-tipster (accessed on August 13, 2010).

xxiv "Cyber crime," *The Daily Star*, July 14, 2010.

xxv "Cyber-crime on the rise, says AIG Tripura," *The Daily Star*, November 5, 2007.

xxvi The complete ICT Act 2006 is available at http://www.bcc.net.bd/Bangla/Acts/ICTAct2009/ict-Act1.htm (accessed on August 19, 2010).

xxvii http://www.thedailystar.net/magazine/2009/11/02/cover.htm (accessed on August 19, 2010).

xxviii Ibid

xxix "Cyber crime," *The Daily Star*, July 14, 2010.

xxx "Bangladesh Police to set up cyber crime unit," *The Daily Star*, November 2, 2007.

xxxi "Microsoft team trains lawmen, officials in cybercrime probes," *Daily New Age*, February 11, 2008.

xxxii "Bangladesh Police to set up cyber crime unit," *The Daily Star*, November 2, 2007.

xxxiii Ishtiaque Alam, "Cyber security and Bangladesh," *Bangladesh Defence Journal*, Issue 37, April 2011, p. 22.

www.ingramcontent.com/pod-product-compliance
Lightning Source LLC
Chambersburg PA
CBHW081239180526
45171CB00005B/475